Migration Law in Ghana

Migration Law in Ghana

Samuel Obeng Manteaw
Ama Fowa Hammond

This book was originally published as a monograph in the International Encyclopaedia of Laws/Migration Law.

Founding Editor: Roger Blanpain
General Editor: Frank Hendrickx
Volume Editor: Helen Oosterom-Staples

Wolters Kluwer

Published by:
Kluwer Law International B.V.
PO Box 316
2400 AH Alphen aan den Rijn
The Netherlands
E-mail: international-sales@wolterskluwer.com
Website: lrus.wolterskluwer.com

Sold and distributed in North, Central and South America by:
Wolters Kluwer Legal & Regulatory U.S.
7201 McKinney Circle
Frederick, MD 21704
United States of America
Email: customer.service@wolterskluwer.com

Sold and distributed in all other countries by:
Air Business Subscriptions
Rockwood House
Haywards Heath
West Sussex
RH16 3DH
United Kingdom
Email: international-customerservice@wolterskluwer.com

Printed on acid-free paper

ISBN 978-94-035-0313-4

e-Book: ISBN 978-94-035-0195-6
web-PDF: ISBN 978-94-035-0243-4

Printed in the United Kingdom.

The Authors

Dr Samuel Obeng Manteaw is a Lecturer at the University of Ghana School of Law. He holds a PhD in Law from the University of Ghana. He also holds two LLM degrees: an LLM degree in Intellectual Property (from The George Washington University Law School) and an LLM degree in Transnational Business Practice from the Pacific McGeorge School of Law. Samuel is a lawyer by profession and earned his Barrister/Solicitor's Certificate from the Ghana School of Law in 2002, and his LLB degree from the University of Ghana.

He has extensive teaching, consultancy, research and publication record on various subjects including Intellectual Property, Patents, E-Commerce, Legal Education, Energy, Mining, Health, among others. He is a Board Member of Ghana's Council for Law Reporting; was a Board member of the International Nuclear Law Association (the first and only African to be so appointed by the global body), a Board member of the Ghana Nuclear Society, and many other organizations. He has been a Visiting Scholar at several prestigious institutions such as the Pacific McGeorge School of Law in California, International Law Institute in Washington DC, University of Dundee in Scotland, North West University in Potchefstroom South Africa, University of South Florida, University of Western Australia.

Samuel consults for governments, international organizations and entities in several countries spanning various continents on intellectual property, legal, commercial, contractual and negotiations aspects of resources development and innovation. He has attended many conferences, facilitated several seminars and workshops; and has a zeal for capacity building and transfer of knowledge. He has recently facilitated and contributed to courses and workshops sponsored by the Government of Ghana, Australian Government, Cameroonian Government, United Nations Economic Commission for Africa, African Mining for Development Centre, International Mining for Development Centre, University of Western Australia, University of Ghana, GTZ, British Council, FAO and several others. He was Lead Consultant for Africa for a Global Project sponsored by Carnegie Foundation; and has been a Judge in the Phillip Jessup International Moot Court Competition in Washington DC; and an Australia Nationally Accredited Mediator.

He has been awarded several scholarships and fellowships including being a Carnegie Scholar, Finnegan Henderson Scholar, Judge Thomas Buergenthal Scholar, Pacific McGeorge Scholar, Dean Rindskopf Parker Scholar, among many other awards. He is also a District Pastor and Trustee of a church with over 3,000 branches in over thirty-three countries. He is the Executive Director of Development Law Clinic, an NGO that uses law to enhance lives through practical legal interventions in livelihoods.

Ama Fowa Hammond is a Lecturer at the University of Ghana School of Law, where she teaches the laws of Contract, Equity, Succession, Family law, and language and study skills. Her research interests are in the broad areas of law and development, legal pluralism, law and colonialism and migration law. Her publications have tended to focus more narrowly on issues relating to law and society, specifically, the relationship between law and social change, and the impact of law on social policy.

She has worked as a consultant for various organizations and governments in the area of intellectual property, constitutional and criminal law. She serves on the editorial committee of the University of Ghana Law journal as an articles editor and also served as a Board member of the Law Reform Commission of Ghana.

Ama Hammond holds a PhD in law from the University of British Columbia, Vancouver, Canada; a Master of Laws degree from Harvard Law School, Massachusetts, USA; a Bachelor of Laws degree (first-class honours) from the University of Ghana; a Bachelor of Arts degree (first-class honours) from the University of Cape Coast-Ghana; and a Qualifying Certificate for the Practice of Law from the Ghana School of Law.

Table of Contents

List of Abbreviations

ACP	African, Caribbean and Pacific States
AU	African Union
CHRAJ	Commission on Human Rights and Administrative Justice
ECOWAS	Economic Community of West African States
EOCO	Economic and Organised Crime Office
GAAS	Ghana Academy of Arts and Sciences
GFZB	Ghana Free Zones Board
GIPC	Ghana Investment Promotion Centre
GIS	Ghana Immigration Service
GLSS	Ghana Living Standards Survey
GRB	Ghana Refugee Board
GSS	Ghana Statistical Service
ILO	International Labour Organization
IRF	Initial Registration Form
ISSER	Institute of Statistical, Social and Economic Research
KIA	Kotoka International Airport
OAU	Organisation of African Unity
OECD	Organisation for Economic Co-operation and Development
PNDC	Provisional National Defence Council
UNHCR	United Nations High Commissioner for Refugees

List of Abbreviations

List of Tables

List of Tables

Preface

Ghana, a West African English-speaking country with a population of about 23.8 million, has over a hundred ethno-linguistic groups which are further subdivided into numerous cultural and linguistic units. Ghana has had a long history and tradition of population mobility which predates colonial rule. The concept of migration, internal and international with its attendant notions of 'stranger,' 'visitor,' 'alien,' '*hho*,' etc. are well known in Ghana's customary and formal legal frameworks. Six phases of international migration in Ghana may be identified as follows: (1) pre-colonial era; (2) colonial era; (3) 1960s or the immediate post-independence period; (4) 1970–1980; (5) 1980–1990 and (6) 1990 to present. Ghana has detailed laws and regulations on migration and has ratified several international laws on migration. The *Ghana Immigration Service* is the main institution responsible for managing and administering migration matters in Ghana. It works with several other government ministries, departments and agencies.

Data on migration is however not always made available by the relevant institutions in Ghana. It is thus difficult to collect existing information on migration in Ghana. A much-used source of migration data is the Ghana Immigration Service (GIS). Though GIS does not publish its data, relevant data on different aspects of migration in Ghana is obtainable on request from an information desk at the GIS headquarters in Accra. The data collected by GIS focuses on the immigration and emigration of both Ghanaians and non-Ghanaians into and out of Ghana. The data is mainly collected at ports and official land entry points. So the GIS data is less reliable for documenting trans-border migrants who use clandestine routes across borders. The GIS data is probably more useful for documenting movements of non-Africans, but even then, it does not accurately distinguish between types of international movement (tourist and migrants). Many other sources of migration data exist, but they often use a small sample frame, do not have a nationwide coverage and are thus qualitative, not statistically representative. Some of these sources contain very dated data with very infrequent updates.

Data or statistical figures on migration in Ghana or a database upon which one can build or update already existing information on migration are lacking and generally unavailable in Ghana. Often, only estimates could be given as to the number of emigrants or immigrants from or in Ghana at any given period (Manuh, 2006). This can be partially attributed to the fact that migration information has not been collected systematically and extensively by the relevant institutions: embassies, Ministry of Interior, GIS, GSS, etc. which has contributed to this state of affairs. Notwithstanding the gaps in migration data in Ghana, the data from the relevant institutions, especially the GIS, does provide a good overview of immigrants and emigrants with regular status and their entry into and exit out of Ghana. Thus, an improvement in migration data capturing processes will really complement Ghana's very detailed laws and regulations on several aspects of migration in Ghana.

General Introduction

§1. Immigration History and Statistical Information

I. Immigration History

1. Located in West Africa, Ghana shares borders with the Gulf of Guinea (south), Burkina Faso (north), Cote d'Ivoire (west) and Togo (east). Ghana covers an area of 239,460 km^2 and is an English-speaking country, but is comprised of about a hundred ethno-linguistic groups, which are further subdivided into numerous cultural and linguistic units, giving Ghana a unique cultural diversity. Ghana's greatest assets are its people (about 23.8 million) who are renowned for their warmth and hospitality. Heralded as a shining example of democratization and good governance in Africa, Ghana's major foreign exchange earners include minerals (mostly gold and diamond), agricultural produce (especially cocoa), and foreign remittances. Ghana also exports a lot of timber and has an active tourism industry being the home of several tourist attractions such as forts and castles, large lakes, rivers and game parks. A recent off shore oil find is now generating significant international commercial interest in Ghana. Ghana has had a long history and tradition of population mobility which predates colonial rule. Six phases of international migration in Ghana may be identified as follows:

(1) Pre-colonial era.
(2) Colonial era.
(3) 1960s or period immediately following independence.
(4) 1970–1980.
(5) 1980–1990.
(6) 1990 to present.

2. During the first phase, the pre-colonial era, people moved from one territorial location to settle elsewhere (seasonally, in transit and permanently) in search of well-being. Factors that fuelled migration included nomadism (seasonal migration), share-cropping or ecological migration, trans-Saharan trade in salt, gold, etc., quest for security, flight from wars and raids following trading in slaves (both trans-Saharan and trans-Atlantic), and the 'free' movement of individuals and families in search of livelihoods. The *Soninké* ethnic group which contributed to the creation of the Ghana Empire were a very mobile trading people, and they established trading centres, and criss-crossed all the major commercial hubs of West Africa. These historical migratory movements in Africa were often dense, and across borders that were wide open. These borders still pose problems for African countries including Ghana where national construction only commenced in the late 1950s or 1960s after independence.

3. In the second phase, the colonial era, Ghana continued to experience various forms of migration and population mobility: people were posted from one colony to the other as colonial assistants, public service officers, civil servants, workers, infantry soldiers, etc. There were also migrations of Mossi and other Burkinabe migrants into Ghana from the colonial period up to the late 1960s to work on southern cocoa farms, because Ghana is a zone of relative lush endowment. It was in this way that countries in the West African Sahel fed into Ghana's position as a major producer of cocoa for the world market. Addo (1974) attributed the success of the cocoa industry in Ghana to the availability of cheap labour from interior countries. There were male traders from Mali and Niger who controlled wholesale trade in grains, cereals and dry goods such as onions in markets in Ghana (Clark 1994).

4. In 1957, Ghana became the first sub-Saharan country to achieve independence and became a Republic in 1960. In this third phase, Ghana was a country of net immigration and played host to Africans from the West African sub-region until late 1960s (Anarfi et al, 2003; Eades 1987, 1993; Schildkrout 1975, 1979; Sudarkassa 1975, 1979). There was little Ghanaian international migration which was mainly for education, training, trading and foreign services (Anarfi et al, 2003). Most people migrated to receive training in order to play critical role in the development of the newly independent country. During this phase, Ghana had minimal emigration and was rather a country of immigration. According to Zachariah and Conde (1981), 12% of the total population of Ghana was of foreign origin in 1960. The in-flow was interrupted during the tailend of the third phase in the late 1960s, and at the beginning of the fourth phase. In 1970, the alien population in Ghana had decreased from 12% of the 1960s to 6.6%. This drop in Ghana's alien population was mainly attributable to the enactment of the *Aliens' Compliance Order* in 1969 (Zachariah and Conde, 1981). The *Aliens Compliance Order* required all aliens in Ghana to obtain the relevant permits within two weeks or otherwise face expulsion. This led to the first and the largest deportation exercise in Ghana, affecting hundreds of thousands of mostly migrant Africans from the neighbouring countries of Togo, Benin (then Dahomey), La Cote d'Ivoire, Burkina Faso (then Upper Volta), Niger, Mali and Nigeria. The *Aliens' Compliance Order*, directed at West African nationals, effectively stemmed the tide of immigration into Ghana for decades.

5. The fourth phase (the decade 1970–1980) also witnessed a sharp rise in international emigration among Ghanaians. This was due to the economic hardship that Ghana experienced in the late 1970s. Due to economic difficulties, Ghanaian professionals including teachers, lecturers, lawyers, administrators, etc. emigrated to sister African countries like Botswana, Nigeria (with its oil boom at that time), Uganda and Zambia where their services were in high demand (Anarfi et al, 2003). Between 1974 and 1981, about two million Ghanaians left the country and the highly skilled formed a significant proportion of those leaving Ghana (Rimmer, 1993). The alien population of Ghana continued to decrease, and by 1984, it had reduced from the 1970 estimates of 6.6%–3.1%. Although this was mainly due to the 1969*Aliens' Compliance Order*, the economic hardship in the country at the time also had its toll.

6. By the fifth phase (1980–1990), emigration had become a coping strategy for individuals and families. The period saw large-scale emigration of Ghanaians: unskilled, semi-skilled and highly skilled labour (Anarfi et al, 2000). During this era, emigration of Ghanaians to Cote d'Ivoire and Nigeria was phenomenal. The economic decline resulted in the fall in real wages, shortage of basic goods and services, high inflation (van Hear, 1998) and led to departures from Ghana. Coincidentally, cross-border movements within West Africa were boosted by the enactment of the Economic Community of West African States (ECOWAS) Protocol on free movement of persons, residence and establishments in 1979. Besides labour migrants, some citizens fled Ghana for fear of political persecution, confiscation of property, imprisonment without trials, executions, as a 'revolutionary' military regime took power from 1981–1992. According to Bump (2006), United Nations High Commissioner for Refugees (UNHCR) registered over 90,000 Ghanaian asylum seekers for the period 1982–1991, making Ghana one of the top ten countries of origin of forced migration at that time (EU, 2006).

7. The sixth phase (1990s to date) has seen some emigration of Ghanaians to Europe and North America. But emigration within West Africa and to other African countries remains the most important, in terms of volume. Generally, however, Ghanaian emigrants are dispersed across the globe. Van Hear (1998) estimates that the Ghanaian Diaspora is currently among the ten new Diasporas globally since the 1990s. This period has seen migration among all categories of persons including the unskilled, the semi-skilled and the skilled. The exodus of people from Ghana may be attributed to poverty, poor educational opportunities, poor health care, inadequate salaries in the public sector that have failed to keep up with inflation, failure of civil service pay reform, lack of job opportunities in the private sector and the lure of 'green pastures' mentality which is fuelled by the ostensible affluence of some 'returnees'.

II. Statistical Information

A. Sources and Reliability/Validity of Migration Data in Ghana

8. Adequate empirical migration data is essential for a better understanding of migration issues. But data is not always made available by the relevant institutions in Ghana. It is thus difficult to collect existing information on migration in Ghana. A much-used source of migration data is the Ghana Immigration Service (GIS). GIS does not publish its data, but relevant data on different aspects of migration in Ghana is obtainable on request from an information desk at the GIS headquarters in Accra. The data collected by GIS focuses on the immigration and emigration of both Ghanaians and non-Ghanaians into and out of Ghana. The data mainly collected at ports and official land entry points is less reliable for documenting trans-border migrants who use clandestine routes across borders. The GIS data is probably more useful for documenting movements of non-Africans, but even then it does not accurately distinguish between types of international movement (tourist and migrants).

9. The GIS and the concerned ministries and departments do not register the number of permanent labour immigrants in Ghana, and, therefore, no national statistics are available. However, there are indications that there are permanent labour immigrants in Ghana who have mainly come from the West and Central African sub-region, South Africa, Canada, Australia, the United Kingdom (UK), the United States of America (US), Asia, especially Korea, India, Lebanon, and also more recently, China. Likewise, the data collected by GIS does not reflect the number of immigrants who may be residing in the country illegally. It also does not provide information on the number of Ghanaian emigrants living abroad. As GIS data is not aggregated on the basis of important demographic characteristics such as sex, age, marital status, occupation, educational attainment as such it does not allow a meaningful analysis of the data. Notwithstanding the gaps in the data provided by GIS, it nevertheless provides a good overview of immigrants and emigrants with regular status and their entry to and exit out of Ghana.

10. Another source of migration data is the Ghana Living Standards Surveys (GLSS) of the World Bank and the Ghana Statistical Service (GSS). But, the survey was last conducted in 1998 or 1999 and as such its 'current' information on migration in Ghana is quite dated. Also studies conducted by foreign countries on stocks of Ghanaian migrants in their countries constitute a source of migration data. But these data are collected at ports and/or official entry points and may not reflect the number of Ghanaian immigrants or emigrants who left or entered the countries clandestinely. It also has gaps in the exact number of migrants in those countries who have not regulated their status or who may be residing in those countries illegally.

11. Several ad hocstudies provide data on migration in Ghana, but such studies often use a small sample frame, do not have a nationwide coverage, and are thus qualitative and not statistically representative. Examples are the studies conducted by the Centre for Migration Studies of the University of Ghana, the Development Research Center on Migration, Globalization and Poverty of the University of Sussex, Ministries of State such as the Ministry of Finance and Economic Planning in Ghana, as well as by individual researchers, academics and authors. As Manuh (2006) notes in her *Ghana Migration Profile*, 'there is a general paucity of data or statistical figures on migration in Ghana and a lack of an existing database upon which one can build or update already existing information. At best, only estimates could be given as to the possible number of emigrants or immigrants from/in Ghana at any given period. For instance, a few African embassies contacted could only provide estimates or indirect inferences on the number of their nationals in Ghana since there has not been any systematic way of capturing this information and/or the nationals had not registered with them'.

B. Statistical Figures and Data on Migration in Ghana

12. This monograph relies on the GIS and other credible sources for data on migration in Ghana, including the *Ghana Migration Profile* study which was sponsored by Ghana's Ministry of Finance and Economic Planning. That study relied on a variety of sources to provide detailed and comprehensive statistical information on migration in Ghana (Manuh, 2006). These sources include GIS, GSS, World Bank, EU, Embassies, Centre for Migration Studies of the University of Ghana, the Development Research Center on Migration, Globalization and Poverty of the University of Sussex, various published and unpublished research studies, etc. The *Ghana Migration Profile* study (2006) is a bit dated but remains one of the few 'current' authoritative comprehensive compilations of migration data and statistics in Ghana. This monograph has culled data from the GIS, the *Ghana Migration Profile* study and many other sources to provide extensive information, statistical data and figures on migration in Ghana.

Statistical Information on Immigrants in Ghana

13. The total number of immigrants in Ghana as of2006 was 614,000, representing 2.78% of the total population of 22,113,000 (GIS, 2006 cited in Manuh, 2006). Of the total number of immigrants, 50.8% were male, 48.2% were female and 42% were minors (GIS, 2006 cited in Manuh, 2006). They came from various regions of all five continents (GSS cited in Quartey, 2006 and further cited in Manuh, 2006). Ghana hosts both refugees, the majority of whom have a prima facie status, and asylum seekers fleeing civil wars in Liberia (since 1989), Sierra Leone (since the early 1990s) and Côte d'Ivoire (since 2002).

14. At its peak, the country provided refuge to over 150,000 persons in 1993 (Anarfi et al, 2003; Bump, 2006; both cited in Manuh, 2006), and the total number of persons of concern to UNHCR as of 31 December 2005 was 58,700 (UNHCR, 2008). The GIS count of refugees in 2006 represented 0.22% of the total population. The proportion of females and minors among refugee populations in Ghana has been generally higher than that of males. Two major settlements and some reception centres have been set up in Ghana to house refugees, with the Buduburam camp hosting mostly Liberians, while the Krisan settlement in the Western Region of Ghana (about 300 km from Accra) houses a relatively smaller number of refugees of mixed origin (Table 1).

15. As regards permanent labour immigrants in Ghana, there are no available national statistics since the concerned ministries and departments do not keep figures on their number. However, there are indications that they exist in the country. Many of these migrants come from the WestandCentral African sub-region, South Africa, Canada, Australia, the UK, the US and Asia including Korea, India and Lebanon. For instance, Manuh (2006) cites immigration data estimates from various embassies as follows: 'the Embassy of Niger in Accra estimated that there were 1 million Nigerien nationals residing in Ghana in 2006. This figure represents 8.3 percent of the total Nigerien population of 12 million. Also, the Embassy of Burkina

Faso in Accra estimated that there were 1.5 million Burkinabes residing in Ghana as at 2006. The Embassy of Mali in Accra estimated that there were about 1.5 million Malians residing in Ghana as at 2006'.

16. There are also many temporary and seasonal labour migrants in Ghana, such as Fulani cattle raisers and herders, as well as seasonal workers from Burkina Faso, Niger and Mali who possess a range of skills and are engaged in variety of occupations of low and medium skills such as farming, petty trading, currency changing, day working and gardening (Table 2). Mining and other companies also bring in engineers, technicians and persons with specific skills on short to medium term contracts. These persons come from South Africa, Canada, Australia, the UK and the US. There is also a long tradition of Korean companies engaged in fishing in Ghana which bring in Korean and other Asian nationals.

Table 1 Total Number of International Arrivals in Ghana (1996–2005)

Year	*KIA*	*AFLAO*	*ELUBO*	*PAGA*	*Other Points*	*Total*
1996	130,673	35,101	90,652	44,872		301,298
1997	201,457	32,155	91,543	44,092		369,274
1998	344,080	49,537	76,000	21,914		491,531
1999	231,309	78,906	67,704	24,015		402,024
2000	259,825	90,465	90,323	4,819	10,843	456,275
2001	370,307	95,643	25,571	9,007	9,294	609,822
2002	322,701	80,893	61,997	8,004	10,734	584,329
2003	402,847	48,269	217,128	10,364	10,362	688,961
2004	436,738	43,946	85,299	7,990	8,135	582,108
2005	338,063	25,825	22,144	3,222	3,200	392,481

Source: GIS, 2006 (cited in Manuh, 2006).

Table 2 Arrivals in Ghana by Region of Residence or Origin (1999–2002)

Region	*1999*	*2000*	*2001*	*2002*
Africa	61,001	181,680	323,371	191,274
Benin	1,161	14,474	24,447	5,445
Burkina Faso	3,842	1,917	9,755	9,603
Cote d'Ivoire	3,935	18,687	33,865	6,191
Ghana	26,315	85,683	128,201	110,376
Guinea	1,009	2,790	4,437	1,276
Liberia	2,717	5,932	16,343	4,898

Mali	1,103	2,677	4,965	2,177
Niger	297	1,268	16,429	3,953
Nigeria	8,891	28,489	44,929	24,718
Senegal	726	1,063	2,512	1,375
Sierra Leone	1,370	1,919	3,074	2,951
South Africa	1,977	2,270	3,100	3,625
Togo	1,847	5,906	21,681	5,643
Other Africa	5,811	8,605	9,633	9,043
Asia	9,772	9,916	14,826	17,209
China	964	1,445	1,962	2,511
India	2,942	2,586	4,737	4,752
Lebanon	1,696	1,558	2,826	3,531
Other Asia	4,170	4,317	5,301	6,415
Europe	33,912	37,690	58,535	63,876
Austria	479	366	767	725
France	3,539	2,912	5,215	4,270
Germany	6,914	6,064	7,810	9,161
Italy	1,916	2,479	1,928	2,421
The Netherlands	7,212	6,682	8,197	10,498
United Kingdom	6,400	11,589	23,330	23,969
Other Europe	7,452	7,571	11,288	12,805
LAC	846	783	1,172	1,851
North America	6,288	16,572	33,093	39,056
Canada	2,888	2,969	4,361	4,650
United States	3,400	13,603	28,421	34,402
Other North America	-	-	311	4
Oceania	982	1,485	1,808	1,734
Total	**112,801**	**242,126**	**432,805**	**315,000**

Source: GSS, 2005 (in Quartey, 2006& Twum-Baah, 2005).

17. Information gathered from embarkation and disembarkation cards (GIS Form 14) in 2006is summarily analysed in Table 3:

Table 3 Arrivals and Departures (Embarkation and Disembarkation) in 2006

	Arrival	*Departure*

Total (Number of Migrants in 2006)	508,199	528,948
Ghanaian Migrants (% of total migrants)	33%	37%
ECOWAS Migrants (% of total migrants)	26%	23%
Other Migrants (% of total migrants)	41%	40%
Total Migrants (% of total migrants)	100%	100%
Deficit (Ghanaian Migrants)	-	4% (37%–33%)
Deficit (ECOWAS & Other Migrants)	4% (67%–63%)	-
1st Quarter (% of total migrants)	23%	23%
2nd Quarter (% of total migrants)	23%	24%
3rd Quarter (% of total migrants)	28%	28%
4th Quarter (% of total migrants)	26%	25%
KIA (Kotoka Int'l Airport in Accra)	80%	78%
AFLAO (Ghana-Togo Border)	8%	9%
ELUBO (Ghana-Cote d'Ivoire Border)	8%	8%
PAGA (Ghana-Burkina Faso Border)	2%	2%
OTHER Entry/Exit Points in Ghana	2%	3%

Source: GSS, 2009.

18. In 2006, 528,948 persons entered and 508,199 left Ghana using the approved entry and exit points. Around 33% of the arrivals and 37% of the departures were Ghanaian migrants. ECOWAS migrants recorded 26% of the total of arrivals and 23% of the total departures. Other migrants constituted 41% of the total of arrivals and 40% of the total of departures. Arrival figures for non-Ghanaians exceeded the departure figures, meaning that the percentage of non-Ghanaians that entered the country was 4% higher than that for Ghanaians entering the country. Conversely departure figures for Ghanaians exceeded the figures of non-Ghanaians entering the country, meaning that more Ghanaians than non-Ghanaians (4%) left the country. In the first quarter of 2006, 23% of total arrivals and 23% of the total departures were recorded. There was no change in arrivals for the second quarter. However, there was a 1% increase in departures. The third quarter witnessed a sharp increase in both arrivals and departures; by 5% each compared to first quarter. Finally, in the fourth quarter, 26% of the annual arrivals and 25% of the annual departures were recorded. Comparing the third and fourth quarters of 2006, there was a 2% decrease in arrivals and a 3% decrease in departures. The collected data was further categorized into entry/exit points including the four major points (KIA, AFLAO, ELUBO and PAGA) and the other entry/exit points (all stations apart from the four major stations). KIA recorded the highest figures for the year representing 80% of the total number of arrivals and 78% of the total number of departures, followed by Aflao with 8% of the total number of arrivals and 9% of the total number of departures. Elubo followed closely with 8% of the total number of arrivals and 8% of the total number of departures. Paga had 2% of the total number of arrivals and 2% of the total number of departures. Finally, the other entry/exit points together had 2% of the total number of arrivals and 3% of the total number of departures.

19. In 2007, 580,895 travellers arrived in Ghana and 621,564 people departed from Ghana. Ghanaian migrants constituted 33.71% of the total number of arrivals and 36.10% of the total number of departures. ECOWAS migrants recorded 28.27% of the arrivals and 25.67% of the departures and other migrants recorded 38.02% and 38.23% of the total number of arrivals and departures, respectively. Many of the migrants used the Kotoka International Airport (KIA) in Accra (77.97% of the total number of arrivals and 77.26% of the total number of departures). This was followed by Elubo with 10.08% of the total number of arrivals and 9.36% of the total number of departures, Aflao with 7.80% of the total number of arrivals and 8.72% of the total number of departures and Paga with 2.21% of the total number of arrivals and 2.09% of the total number of departures. The other entry/exit points had 1.94% of the total number of arrivals and 2.57% of the total number of departures. In January the lowest number of arrivals was recorded, namely 4.36%, while August recorded 10.76% of the yearly arrivals, making it the month with the highest number in total arrivals for the period under review. February and August showed the lowest and highest figures in total departure, respectively, 6.43% and 11.27%. With the highest number of both arrivals and departures, the month of August can be attributed to the celebration of 'PANAFRICAN FESTIVAL' with a lot of people, including Africans in the Diaspora, visiting the country. The information gathered from embarkation and disembarkation cards (GIS Form 14) in 2007, therefore, is summarily analysed in Table 4:

Table 4 Arrivals and Departures (Embarkation and Disembarkation) in 2007

	Arrival	*Departure*
Total (Number of Migrants in 2007)	580,895	621,564
Ghanaian Migrants (% of total migrants)	33.71%	36.10%
ECOWAS Migrants (% of total migrants)	28.27%	25.67%

Other Migrants (% of total migrants)	38.02%	38.23%
Total Migrants (% of total migrants)	100%	100%
Deficit (Ghanaian Migrants)	-	2.39% (36.10%–33.71%)
Deficit (ECOWAS & Other Migrants)	2.39% (66.29%–63.9%)	-
Month of August (Highest Migration)	10.76%	11.27%
KIA (Kotoka Int'l Airport, Accra)	77.97%	77.26%
AFLAO (Ghana-Togo Border)	7.80%	8.72%
ELUBO (Ghana-Cote d'Ivoire Border)	10.08%	9.36%
PAGA (Ghana-Burkina Faso Border)	2.21%	2.09%
OTHER Entry/Exit Points in Ghana	1.94%	2.57%

Source: GSS, 2009.

Table 5 indicates an increase in 2008 over the 2007 figures for both arrivals (15.76%) and departures (12.86%).

Table 5 Arrivals and Departures (Embarkation and Disembarkation) in 2008

	Arrival	*Departure*
Total (Number of Migrants in 2008)	672,434	701,493
Ghanaian Migrants (Number of Migrants)	211,985	234,791
Ghanaian Migrants (% of total migrants)	31.53%	33.47%
ECOWAS Migrants (Number of Migrants)	204,868	200,444
ECOWAS Migrants (% of total migrants)	30.47%	28.57%
Other Migrants (Number of Migrants)	255,581	266,258
Other Migrants (% of total migrants)	38.01%	37.96%

Total Migrants (% of total migrants)	100%	100%
Deficit (Ghanaian Migrants)	-	1.94% (33.47%–31.53%)
Deficit (ECOWAS & Other Migrants)	1.95% (68.48%–66.53%)	-
Month of August (Highest Migration)	70,128 (10.43%)	72,230 (10.30%)
KIA (Kotoka International Airport, Accra)	77.85% (523,508)	76.08% (543,414)
AFLAO (Ghana-Togo Border)	7.40% (49,740)	8.17% (57,282)
ELUBO (Ghana-Cote d'Ivoire Border)	10.35% (71,408)	10.24% (67,737)
PAGA (Ghana-Burkina Faso Border)	2.01% (13,487)	1.92% (13,502)
OTHER Entry/Exit Points in Ghana	2.13% (14,291)	2.79% (19,558)

Source: GSS, 2009.

Statistical Information on Emigrants

20. There is no official accurate figure for the number of Ghanaians living outside Ghana, so the volume of emigration is based on estimates. While both the GSS and the GIS collect data on Ghanaians leaving the country through the approved departure points, they do not have data on Ghanaians living abroad as they generally do not register with the embassies abroad.

21. The GSS estimated 1,373,089 departures between 1999 and 2002. The GIS in 2006 estimated a total of 4,118,966 departures from Ghana between 1996 and 2005. Tables 3, 4 and 5 show the departure and arrival of Ghanaians from 2000 to 2008. A total of 153,632 Ghanaians left the country but did not return during the period 2000–2007 (*see* Table 7). This represents 0.67% of the total population of 22,900,927 (2008 mid-year estimate by GSS). Data from GIS for this period reveals that with the exception of 2003 and 2004, there has been consistent rise in the number of Ghanaians who travelled abroad.

22. As shown in Table 3, in 2006, 528,948 persons arrived in Ghana and 508,199 left the country using approved entry and exit points. Ghanaian migrants constituted 33% of the total number of arrivals and 37% of the total number of departures. Thus, 4% of the Ghanaian travellers in 2006 emigrated from the country that year. Table 5 indicates an increase in the number of arrivals and departures in 2007 compared to 2006. In 2007, 580,895 travellers arrived in Ghana and 621,564 people departed from the country. Ghanaian migrants constituted 33.71% of the total number of arrivals and 36.10% of the total number of departures. Thus, 2.39% of Gha naian travellers in 2007 emigrated from the country that year. In 2008, there was an increase of 12.86% over the 2007 figures for departures. Of the 701,493 people who left Ghana, 324,791 (33.47%) were Ghanaians and 1.94% of them did not return that year.

23. In 2000, World Bank[1] estimates based on UNDP's 2,000 population data indicated that 906,698 Ghanaians, representing 4.5% of the total Ghanaian population, were emigrants. Peil (1995) has estimated that by the 1990s, 10%–20% of Ghana's population lived abroad. It has been observed that Ghana had a place in the top ten emigration countries in sub-Saharan Africa in 2005 (EU, 2006 cited in Manuh, 2006). By early 2000, Ghana had an emigration rate of 42.9% for the tertiary educated and was ranked seventh among the top ten sub-Saharan Africa (EU, 2006). It is estimated that in 2006 there were about 189,461 Ghanaian migrants living in Organisation for Economic Co-operation and Development (OECD) countries. This number represents 0.86% of the Ghanaian population namely 22,113,000 (OECD, 2006). Of the 189,461 Ghanaian migrants in the OECD countries, 25.3% were citizens of their respective countries of residence, 44.9% lived as foreigners, while the remaining 29.8% had unknown status. Of these, the US had the largest share of Ghanaian emigrants, about 35.5% (67,190), followed by the UK (29.6%, 56,112), Italy (9.2%, 17,471), Canada (9%, 17,071), the Netherlands (5.9%, 11,201) and France (2.3%, 4,376) (OECD, 2006).

24. The main countries of destination of Ghanaian emigrants are the US, the UK, Canada, Germany, Italy, Nigeria, Botswana and South Africa (GIS 2006). Other secondary sources add the following countries to the list of main destination countries: Cote D'Ivoire, Togo, Burkina Faso, Gambia, Sierra Leone, Benin and the Netherlands (Twum-Baah, 2005; Bump, 2006; Anarfi et al, 2003). Regarding the rate of return, the divide between temporary and permanent migration is not easy to establish. While many Ghanaians remain abroad permanently, an increasingly substantial number are returning to Ghana. Some of those who return maintain a desire to re-emigrate, so their return should not be regarded as permanent (Twum-Baah 2005). Table 6 gives estimates of Ghanaians living in some developed countries.

Table 6 Ghanaian Emigrants by Country

Country	*Emigrants*	*Year*
UK[1]	96,650	2006
USA[2]	67,190	2000
Italy[3]	34,499	2005
Germany[4]	20,636	2004
Canada[5]	17,070	2001

1. Peter Quartey, *Ghana, in Remittance Markets in Africa* 133–153, 137 (Sanket Mohapatra & Dilip Ratha, The World Bank 2011). Online: http://siteresources.worldbank.org/EXTDECPROSPECTS/Resources/476882-1157133580628/RMA_FullReport.pdf.

The Netherlands[6]	12,196	2007
Spain[7]	12,068	2006
France[8]	4,096	1999

1. Labour Force Survey 2006 (UK).
2. Census Bureau, 2000 (USA).
3. At www.istat.it (Italy).
4. Federal Statistical Office, 2004 (Germany).
5. Canadian Citizenship and Immigration Office 2001.
6. At www.cbc.nl (The Netherlands).
7. At www.ines.es (Spain).
8. At www.ined.fr (France).

Table 7 Annual Arrivals and Departures of Ghanaians (2000–2007)

Year	*Arrival*	*% of Population*	*Departures*	*% of Population*
2000	85,683	0.45	110,718	0.59
2001	128,201	0.68	121,159	0.64
2002	110,376	0.58	158,212	0.84
2003	145,878	0.77	143,367	0.76
2004	136,766	0.72	139,349	0.74
2005	125,594	0.66	151,716	0.80
2006	162,624	0.86	162,624	1.04
2007	195,817	1.04	224,372	1.19
Total	1,090,972	5.77	1,244,604	6.59
Deficit	-	-	*153,632*	*0.67*

Source: GIS, 2008.

25. Ghanaian labour emigrants are mainly from the health and educational sectors. In the health sector, it is estimated that more Ghanaian doctors are working outside than in Ghana. The country has lost 50% of its professional nurses to the UK, US and Canada. Estimated vacancy levels in Ghana's Health Service in 2002 for doctors was 65%, for professional nurses 68% and for pharmacists 56.6%. The estimated brain drain of health workers (doctors, pharmacists, nurses/midwives and allied health workers) for the period 1999–2004 totalled 2,094 (MoH, in Nyonator and Dovlo, 2005). An estimated 15% of Ghanaians with higher education has emigrated to the US and a further 10% to other OECD countries, leading to a shortage of lecturers in Ghana's higher educational institutions (Carrington and Detragiache,

1998, cited in Black 2003; Manuh et al. 2005). Other activities Ghanaian emigrants engage in are: professional, managerial and administrative as well as domestic services.

Table 8 Departures from Ghana by Region of Residence or Origin (1999–2002)

	Departures			
Region	*1999*	*2000*	*2001*	*2002*
AFRICA	143,109	225,448	288,329	224,845
Benin	8,936	9,469	20,211	3,378
Burkina Faso	3,440	10,044	4,536	2,669
Cote d'Ivoire	12,083	11,168	30,043	3,873
Ghana	75,843	110,718	121,159	158,212
Guinea	1,120	2,040	3,990	2,363
Liberia	3,549	7,575	11,845	6,757
Mali	1,588	2,948	3,152	1,875
Niger	943	759	4,784	1,978
Nigeria	20,005	40,753	53,884	22,768
Senegal	1,017	927	1,860	1,536
Sierra Leone	1,220	1,812	3,205	3,173
South Africa	1,1415	2,458	3,113	2,844
Togo	6,903	13,885	16,420	4,457
Other Africa	5,047	10,892	9,767	8,932
ASIA	7,328	12,118	15,000	18,296
China	1,325	1,684	1,945	1,706
India	1,830	3,116	3,848	6,271
Lebanon	1,120	1,588	2,807	5,278
Other Asia	3,053	5,730	6,400	5,041
EUROPE	33,425	56,558	46,846	61,124
Austria	436	5,705	611	481
France	2,628	4,658	4,750	4,757
Germany	4,619	5,844	6,368	6,817
Italy	1,550	3,054	1,900	2,035
The Netherlands	4,172	6,191	6,146	10,240
United Kingdom	13,734	20,957	16,476	26,166
Other Europe	6,286	9,421	10,595	10,628
LAC	762	988	1,297	1,051

NORTH AMERICA	22,688	120,216	26,698	36,812
Canada	2,976	3,887	4,270	4,568
United States	19,705	116,322	22,403	32,225
Other North America	7	7	25	19
OCEANIA	1,585	25,102	1,903	1,561
TOTAL	**208,897**	**440,430**	**380,073**	**343,689**

Source: GSS, 2005 (cited in Awumbila et al., 2008, p. 10; Twum-Baah, 2005; Manuh, 2006).

Table 9 Total Number of International Departures from Ghana (1996–2005)

Year	*KIA*	*AFLAO*	*ELUBO*	*PAGA*	*OTHER POINTS*	*TOTAL*
1996	195,585	15,000	73,969	10,279		294,833
1997	209,761	35,445	74,146	35,777		355,129
1998	354,615	53,997	68,794	20,860		498,266
1999	266,773	67,188	65,125	19,817		418903
2000	293,518	92,234	73,224	5,038	13,172	477,186
2001	217,198	75,012	102,597	5,989	6,976	407,772
2002	329,416	78,512	71,948	4,884	7,978	492,738
2003	234,030	30,505	105,639	8,444	8,859	387,477
2004	246,970	53,368	57,378	8,821	10,083	376,620
2005	359,573	25,590	15,014	3,362	6,503	410,042

Source: GIS, 2006 (cited in Manuh, 2006).

26. Data on emigration rates differentiating between male and female migrants is rather hard to obtain, although efforts are now being made in some sectors to address this gap in the data available. Generally speaking, however, Ghanaian emigrants are more likely to be male than female (Litchfield et al, 2003). The proportion for Ghanaian females actually remains under 40%. The higher proportion (more than 51%) of Ghanaian females than males in Wales and England (1991 and 2001), particularly in the younger ages up to age 44, may reflect a more rapid increase of females and younger persons leaving Ghana to be reunited with their family members (Anarfi et al, 2003). Women also dominate short distance emigration to nearby countries, especially in the sub-region, whereas a higher proportion of men travel further afield (Anarfi et al., 2003). Younger Ghanaian adults are also more likely to migrate than older persons (Manuh, 2006).

27. According to Bump (2006), UNHCR registered over 90,000 Ghanaian asylum seekers for the period 1982–1991, making Ghana one of the top ten countries of origin of forced migration at that time (EU, 2006). However, from 1992 to 2001, Ghana ranked just thirtieth in asylum applications in industrialized countries (Anarfi et al., 2003). Of the EU's estimated 3 million Ghanaian emigrants in 2001, 15,644 were said to be refugees. Around 11,000 Ghanaian refugees were estimated to be in the West African region in 2001, mainly in Togo, with 10,000 remaining in Togo at the end of 2003 (USCR, 2004; UNHCR, 2004). These figures, however, seem inconsistent with the general understanding in Ghana that there are currently no Ghanaian refugee emigrants in developed countries (Tables 8 and 9).

Repatriation of Foreign Nationals and Fraudulent Acquisition of Travel Documents

28. In 2008, a total of 138 foreign nationals were repatriated to their respective countries from Ghana. Their nationalities, the total number of persons per country and the percentage they represent are outlined in Tables 10 and 11, respectively. Data obtained from the KIA by the GIS for 2008 provides the following information of fraudulent acquisition of travelling documents (*see* Table 12).

Table 10 Number of Foreign Nationals Repatriated from Ghana (2008)

Nationality	*Number Repatriated*	*Nationality*	*Number Repatriated*	*Nationality*	*Number Repatriated*
Nigerians	54	Ivoirians	2	Germans	1
Liberians	27	Jordanians	2	Iranians	1
SriLankans	11	Palestinians	2	Mexicans	1
Lebanese	9	Togolese	2	Pakistani	1
Cameroonians	5	Turkish	2	Peruvians	1
Chadians	3	Americans	1	Senegalese	1
Chinese	3	Beninese	1	Swiss	1
Guineans	3	Congolese	1		
Egyptians	2	Dutch	1		

Source: GIS, 2009.

Table 11 Foreign Nationals Repatriated from Ghana (2008) (Percentages)

Nationality	*Percentage Repatriated*	*Nationality*	*Percentage Repatriated*	*Nationality*	*Percentage Repatriated*
Nigerians	38.88%	Ivoirians	1.44%	Germans	0.72%
Liberians	19.44%	Jordanians	1.44%	Iranians	0.72%
SriLankans	7.92%	Palestinians	1.44%	Mexicans	0.72%

Lebanese	6.48%	Togolese	1.44%	Pakistani	0.72%
Cameroonians	3.60%	Turkish	1.44%	Peruvians	0.72%
Chadians	2.16%	Americans	0.72%	Senegalese	0.72%
Chinese	2.16%	Beninese	0.72%	Swiss	0.72%
Guineans	2.16%	Congolese	0.72%		
Egyptians	1.44%	Dutch	0.72%		

Source: GIS, 2009.

Table 12 Fraudulent Acquisition of Travel Documents

Fraudulent Activity	*Percentage*
Photo Substitution	25.72%
Counterfeit Page	15.84%
Impersonation	14.61%
Fraudulent Acquisition of Passport	12.76%
Fraudulent Acquisition of Visa	7.16%
False Endorsement	5.76%
Counterfeit Passport	4.73%
Page Alteration	3.91%
Page Substitution	3.70%
Fraudulent Acquisition of Resident Card	2.26%
Counterfeit Sojourner/Resident Card	1.85%
Proxy Visa	1.23%

Source: GIS, 2009.

§2. Overview of National Legal Instruments

I. Historical Overview

29. The *GIS*, established by the *GIS Law (PNDC Law 226)* in 1989, is the government agency responsible for the enforcement of all statutory and regulatory enactments relating to immigration. The *GIS* started as the *Immigration and Passport Unit of the Gold Coast Colonial Police Force* under the command of Mr Nevile C. Hill. During this period, immigration in Ghana was governed by a Colonial Ordinance and most aliens were colonial civil servants, with a few traders and missionaries, and other West African nationals. On attainment of independence in 1957, the rapid expansion of the economy coupled with Ghana's role as a leader in the African liberation struggle led to an increasing number of foreign businessmen, tourists and African aliens moving into the country. To control this influx and enhance the service to these aliens, in 1960 a Cabinet decision transferred the Immigration Unit to the Ministry of the Interior as a separate department, while the Ministry of Foreign Affairs assumed the task of issuing passports. Regulations such as the *Immigration Regulations, 1959 (L.N. 65)*, and the *Immigration (Amendment) Regulations, 1960 (L.I. 82)* were also adopted to streamline immigration procedures. Three years later, the *Aliens Act 1963 (Act 160)* was enacted to give legal backing to immigration operations in Ghana.

30. *Act160* provided rules on '*Entry into Ghana*', including rules requiring any foreigner arriving in Ghana by sea, land or air to appear before an immigration officer for examination, in accordance with existing requirements prior to entry. Exceptions were, however, made to this rule for persons who arrived by air or sea in direct transit to a third country or, in the case of air travel, who did not leave the precincts of the airport. The Act 160 also provided the immigration officer competence to refuse permission to enter to any person who did not meet the conditions of entry, such as not being in possession of a valid travel document or visa, or being a prohibited immigrant. These rules were intended to achieve several purposes, namely, to secure national frontiers, to control legal immigration, to prevent illegal immigration and its consequences, to promote social cohesion and to facilitate genuine tourism. The Act was also meant to contribute towards establishing a conducive and protected environment for sound business activities.

31. Under *section 10(1) of Act 160*, entitled '*Residence and Employment of Aliens in Ghana*' employers were forbidden from engaging the services of expatriates or aliens resident or working in the country, 'except in accordance with a licence in writing granted by the Minister' through the Immigration Quota System and which can be renewed or revoked. This policy was developed to regulate immigrant activities and protect the indigenous labour market from undue foreign competition and 'plundering' of national resources by 'unscrupulous' aliens. The Act also provided that aliens who intended to stay in the country for longer periods (usually more than a year) as dependents or students were required to apply for residence permits. Aliens who were entitled to work needed both a residence and a work permit and could be guilty of an offence if they breached the conditions on which the permits were issued, such as changing employment or business, being employed without work permit or failing to renew one or both of the permits on expiry. The effect of contravening the Act was became very clear in 1969, when the Government of the Progress Party issued the *Aliens Compliance Order*, which required all aliens in Ghana to obtain the relevant permits within two weeks or face expulsion. This eventually resulted in the largest deportation exercise carried out in Ghana, affecting hundreds of thousands of migrants, mostly Africans from the neighbouring countries of Togo, Benin (then Dahomey), La Cote d'Ivoire, Burkina Faso (then Upper Volta), Niger, Mali and Nigeria.

32. In November 1989, the *GIS Law (PNDC Law 226)* converted the Immigration Department into a paramilitary service that remains the sole institution with a statutory mandate to regulate and monitor the entry, residence, employment and the exit of foreigners in the country. The *Aliens Act, 1963 (Act 160)* and its commencement legislative instrument the *Aliens Act, 1963 (Commencement) Instrument, 1963 (L.I. 247)* were amended several times by among others the *Aliens (Amendment) Act, 1965 (Act 265)* and the *Aliens (Amendment) Decree, 1974, (N.R.C.D. 259)*. The implementing instrument, the *Aliens Regulations, 1963 (L.I. 265)*, was also subject to several amendments, some of the amending acts are the *Aliens (Amendment) Regulations, 1967 (L.I. 553)*, the *Aliens (Amendment) Regulations, 1974 (L.I. 970)*, the *Aliens (Amendment) Regulations, 1977 (L.I. 1103)*, the *Aliens (Amendment) Regulations, 1981 (L.I. 1266)*, the *Immigration (Amendment) Regulations (Revocation) Instrument, 1992 (L.I. 1542)* and the *Aliens (Amendment) Regulations, 1994 (L.I. 1581)*.

33. By the late 1990s, there was the need to update the law on immigration to conform to current developments, policies and Ghana's international obligations under the *Treaty of ECOWAS* and its Protocols, and other international conventions. This led to the adoption of the *Immigration Act, 2000 (Act 573)*. *Act 573* repealed the *Aliens Act, 1963 (Act 160)* and its amendments. In 2001, the *Immigration Regulations, 2001 (L.I. 1691)* was also enacted to revoke and replace the *Aliens Regulations, 1963 (L.I. 265)* and its amendments.

II. Current Applicable Legislation

34. Current principal applicable migration laws in Ghana include:

(1) *Constitution of Ghana, 1992.*
(2) *Immigration Act, 2000 (Act 573).*
(3) *Immigration Regulations, 2001 (L.I. 1691).*
(4) *Immigration Service Law, 1989 (PNDC Law 226).*
(5) *Immigration Service Regulations, 1997 (L.I. 1636).*
(6) *Citizenship Act, 2000 (Act 591).*
(7) *Citizenship Regulations, 2001 (L.I.1690).*
(8) *Refugee Law, 1992 (P.N.D.C.L. 305D).*
(9) *The Ghana Investment Promotion Act, 2013 (Act 865).*
(10) *Ghana Investment Promotion Centre (Tourism) Instrument, 2005 (L.I.1817).*
(11) *The Free Zones Act, 1995 (Act 504).*
(12) *Free Zone (Amendment) Act, 2002 (Act 618).*
(13) *Free Zone Regulations, 1996 (L.I.1618).*
(14) *Internal Revenue Act, 2000 (Act 592).*
(15) *Small Scale Gold Mining Act, 1989 (PNDCL 218).*
(16) *Diamonds Act, 1972 (N.R.C.D. 32).*
(17) *Concessions Act, 1939 (Cap 136) (enacted as Concessions Ordinance, 1939(19)).*
(18) *Criminal Offences Act, 1960 (Act 29)*(originally enacted as *Criminal Code*).
(19) *Children's Act, 1998 (Act 560) and Child Rights Regulations, 2002 (L.I.1705).*

(20) *Labour Act, 2000 (651) and Labour Regulations, 2007 (1833).*
(21) *Human Trafficking Act, 2005 (Act 694).*
(22) *Aliens (Permits for Prohibited Areas) Regulations, 1969 (L.I. 612).*
(23) *Aliens (Permits for Prohibited Areas) (Amendment) Regulations, 1981 (L.I. 1267).*
(24) *Alien Enterprises Licensing Regulations, 1970 (L.I. 670).*
(25) *Aliens (Registration) (Amendment) Regulations, 1974 (L.I. 883).*
(26) *Aliens (Registration) (Amendment) Regulations, 1974 (L.I. 969).*
(27) *Aliens (Registration) (Amendment) Regulations, 1975 (L.I. 1052).*
(28) *Identity Cards Decree, 1972 (N.R.C.D. 129).*
(29) *Identity Cards Regulations, 1972 (L.I. 794).*
(30) *Social Security Regulations, 1973 (L.I. 818).*

35. The *Immigration Act, 2000 (Act 573)* is the key law on immigration in Ghana. It regulates migration issues in Ghana including entry into and departure from the country, residence and employment of foreign nationals in Ghana, the deportation of foreigners, exemption and detention of foreigners, petitions and miscellaneous provisions and offences. Part 1 of the Act covers most of the repealed provisions of *Act 160:* embarkation and disembarkation at approved points and appearance before immigration officers on arrival and departure. Section 4 of the Act sets out the conditions for entry into Ghana and the documents which a potential entrant in Ghana must possess: a valid passport or other travel document and a valid visa or emergency entry permit. Persons who occupy an exempt status do not require entry visa by reason of treaty or other obligation assumed by Ghana. Such exempt persons include nationals of the fifteenmembers of the ECOWAS[2] under the relevant ECOWAS Protocols, Malaysia and Kenya. Although *Act 573* does not make specific provision for ECOWAS citizens, the *Immigration Regulations, 2001 (L.I. 1691)* provide for ECOWAS citizens in *Regulations 3 and 8* thereby ensuring compliance with Ghana's international obligations under the ECOWAS Protocols on migration.[3]*L.I. 1691* was adopted pursuant to the exercise of the powers conferred on the Interior Minister by *section 55* of the *Immigration Act, 2000, (Act 573).* It provides detailed rules on administrative procedures and application forms for implementing *Act 573* including the examination of immigrants and conditions of entry, travel documents, like passport, visa and emergency entry permits, residence permits and the different residential statuses available to immigrants, employment of immigrants, sanctions, etc.

36. Prohibited immigrants are not permitted entry into Ghana. Section 8(1) of *Act 573* defines a prohibited immigrant as follows: 'A person other than a citizen of Ghana is a prohibited immigrant ... if that person (a) has a deportation order in

2. The fifteen members of ECOWAS are: Benin, Burkina Faso, Cape Verde, Cote d'Ivoire, Gambia, Ghana, Guinea, Guinea Bissau, Liberia, Mali, Niger, Nigeria, Senegal, Sierra Leone, and Togo.
3. Under the relevant ECOWAS Treaty and its Protocols as implemented in *Regulations 3 and 8* of the *Immigration Regulations, 2001 (L.I. 1691)*,Ghana grants nationals of ECOWAS Member States admission into the country without any visa requirements whatsoever and provides a maximum of ninety days visitor's permit. It is subject to renewal when an applicant provides reasonable grounds to justify the request for renewal.

force made against him under this Act or any other enactment; (b) is unable to show that he has the means of supporting himself and his dependents if any, or is destitute and likely to be a burden on the public; (c) refuses to submit to a medical examination after being required to do so by a health officer; (d) has been sentenced in a foreign country for any extraditable crime within the Extradition Act of Ghana; (e) has been certified by a health officer to be medically unfit to enter Ghana; (f) has been declared by the Minister by executive instrument to be a person whose entry into Ghana is not conducive to the public good; (g) procures or attempts to bring into Ghana any person for the purpose of prostitution or other immoral purpose; (h) is a person whose activities are contrary to the laws of Ghana; or (i) is the dependent of a person to whom any of the provisions of this sub-section applies.'

37. Act 573 introduces new categories of status, including the *indefinite residence status* (sections 15 and 16) and the *right of abode* (section 17), which may be conferred on migrants. An *indefinite residence status* is conferred on migrants who have stayed in the country for several years[4] and are considered, among others, to have a genuine desire to stay in the country and have made or are 'capable of making a substantial contribution to the development of Ghana'. An indefinite residence status may also be conferred on foreign spouses (i.e., a foreign national married to a Ghanaian citizen), who have less stringent conditions to fulfil.[5] A *right of abode* is conferred on a person who is a Ghanaian by birth, adoption, registration or naturalization within the meaning of the *Citizenship Act, 2000 (Act 591)* but, by reason of the acquisition of a foreign nationality, has lost Ghanaian citizenship. A *right of abode* may also be granted to a person of African descent in the Diaspora.[6] The process of acquisition of Ghanaian citizenship is, however, not governed by *Act 573*, but by Ghana's *1992 Constitution* (more specifically Articles 6–10) and the *Citizenship Act, 2000, (Act 591). Act 591* makes it possible for Ghanaians to keep their Ghanaian citizenship after obtaining the citizenship of another country. The GIS facilitates the implementation of citizenship acquisition processes.

38. The *Immigration Service Law, 1989 (PNDC Law 226)* provides for matters relating to the GIS as highlighted in Article 190(3) of the 1992 Constitution. The *Immigration Service Regulations, 1997 (L.I. 1636)* also set the fees for various permits and revoked the *Aliens (Amendment) Regulations, 1981 (L.I. 1266)*. The adoption of *Immigration Act 2000 (Act 573)* increased the functions and roles of GIS in regulating and monitoring the movement and activities of foreigners in the country.

4. The qualification for the grant of the indefinite residence status are set out in s. 15 of the Act and include residence in Ghana throughout a period of twelve months immediately preceding the date of the application to the Director of Immigration and residence during the seven years immediately preceding that period of twelve months, for an aggregated period of no less than five years.
5. *See* s. 16 of the Act which requires that foreign spouses should have stayed in Ghana for an aggregate period of not more than two years in the twelve months immediately preceding the application. In addition, there is no condition of proving any substantial contribution to the development of Ghana.
6. Among the qualifications for the grant of the status of the right of abode to a person of African descent in the Diaspora are that the person must be of the minimum age of 18, must be of good character, must have independent means, and the ability to contribute substantially to national development.

39. There are several other laws that also regulate immigration in Ghana. The *Identity Cards Regulations, 1972 (L.I. 794)* that implements the *Identity Cards Decree, 1972 (N.R.C.D. 129)* that provides in Regulation 3 that '[unless exempted], every alien of sixteen years and above resident in Ghana shall obtain an identity card in accordance with the provisions of the Decree and these Regulations'. Regulations 4 and 5 of *L.I. 794* further provide respectively that 'No alien resident in Ghana shall be issued with an identity card unless he produces a valid residence permit or is exempted from the need to obtain a residence permit' and that 'No alien who has been issued with an identity card shall change his employment unless he produces his identity card to his new employer.' *The Social Security Regulations, 1973 (L.I. 818)* sets out in its Regulation 51(4) that 'an alien employer may not be permitted to leave Ghana unless he produces to the appropriate immigration authorities a valid Social Security Clearance Certificate issued in respect of his establishment'. The *Internal Revenue Act, 2000 (Act 592)* provides for '*Tax clearance certificates*' in section 118 as follows: 'an alien who has been resident in the Republic or who, not being a person so resident, has a tax liability due under this Act or has income which accrued in or was derived from the Republic with respect to which that alien is chargeable to tax under Sections 1 to 94, shall not depart from the Republic unless that alien produces to the immigration officer at the port of departure a tax clearance certificate'.

40. The Ghana Investment Promotion Act, 2013 (Act 865) and the Free Zones Act, 1995 (Act 504) also have migration related provisions. Act 865 repealed the Ghana Investment Promotion Act 1994 (Act 478) which had before repealed the Ghana Investment Code 1985 (PNDCL 116). Act 865 applies to all sectors and encourages investment by providing a clear and stable institutional framework for investors in Ghana. The Act 865 is extremely important for immigration issues, especially in the field of employment. Under section 27 of Act 865, certain activities are exclusively reserved for Ghanaians. For example, non-Ghanaians are prohibited from sales in markets, petty trading, hawking or selling from kiosks, the operation of taxi and car hire services unless there is a fleet of at least twenty-five new vehicles, offering pool betting services and lotteries, with the exception of football pools, the operation of beauty salons and barber shops, the production of exercise books and other basic stationery, the printing of recharge scratch cards for the use of subscribers of telecommunication services, the retail of finished pharmaceutical products, and the production, supply and retail of sachet water.

41. Section 28 of *Act 865* provides that an enterprise in which foreign participation is permitted shall not be established or operated by a person who is not a citizen unless: (a) in the case of a joint enterprise with a citizen partner, there is an investment by the other person of foreign capital of not less than USD 200,000 in cash or capital goods relevant to the investment or a combination of both by way of equity participation and the partner who is a citizen shall not have less than 10% equity participation in the joint enterprise; or (b) where the enterprise is wholly owned by that person there is an investment of foreign capital of not less than USD 500,000.00 or its equivalent worth in capital goods by way of equity capital. In the case of a trading enterprise involving only the purchasing and selling of goods which is wholly or partly owned by a person who is not a citizen, there shall be an investment of foreign capital or its equivalent in goods worth at least USD 1,000,000 by way of equity capital and the enterprise shall employ at least twenty skilled citizens.

42. Act 865 also provides varying *immigrant quotas* based on the amount of paid-up capital for a foreign enterprise. Section 35 makes provision for *immigrant quotas* as follows:

(1) Every enterprise with a paid-up capital of USD 50,000.00 but less than USD 250,000.00 or its equivalent in cedis shall be entitled to an initial automatic maximum *immigrant quota of one person.*
(2) Every enterprise with a paid-up capital of USD 250,000.00 but less than USD 500,000.00 or its equivalent in cedis shall be entitled to an initial automatic maximum *immigrant quota of two persons.*
(3) Every enterprise with a paid-up capital of USD 500,000.00 but less than USD 700,000.00 or its equivalent in cedis shall be entitled to an initial automatic maximum *immigrant quota of three persons.*
(4) Every enterprise with a minimum paid-up capital of USD 700,000.00 or its equivalent in cedis shall be entitled to an initial automatic maximum *immigrant quota of four persons.*
(5) An enterprise that intends to employ an expatriate shall apply to Ghana Investment Promotion Centre (GIPC) for facilitation of the employment and the application shall specify the number of expatriates to be employed. An application submitted under this section shall be dealt with by the Immigration Service in consultation with the Centre.

43. The *Free Zones Act, 1995 (Act 504)* as amended by the *Free Zone (Amendment) Act, 2002 (Act 618)* provides for the establishment of free zones to aid economic development. It also provides for the regulation of activities in free zones as well as related matters. It focuses on promoting investment in especially the manufacturing sector with the aim of exporting the bulk of the products and provides for the participation of foreign investors in the Free Zones. Section 29 of *Act 504* states that: '(1) a foreign investor may take and hold a maximum of one hundred percent of the shares in a free zone enterprise; (2) a domestic investor may take and hold a maximum of one hundred percent of the shares in an export free zone enterprise; and (3) foreign and domestic investors have equal status within the export free zones'. Section 12 of the Act provides that a person shall not carry on a trade, business or industry within a free zone unless it is registered under (a) the *Companies Act, 1963 (Act 179)*, or (b) the *Incorporated Private Partnerships Act, 1962 (Act 152)*, and holds an incorporated licence authorizing the carrying on of that trade, business or industry under *Act 504.*

44. The *Concessions Act (Ordinance), 1939 (Cap 136)* also has provisions on migration. Section 34(1) of *Cap 136* is entitled *Mining Leases* and provides: 'An alien shall not carry on mining unless the alien is the holder of (a) a concession granting the right to do so from a citizen having the power to grant that right; and

(b) a mining licence from the Minerals Commission … or where the mining is conducted solely by dredging operations, an appropriate dredging licence under the Rivers Act.' Section 19(4) of the *Small Scale Gold Mining Law, 1989 (PNDCL 218)* provides that 'Where an alien is convicted of an offence under this Act the alien is liable after paying the fine or serving the imprisonment imposed to deportation (under the Immigration Act, 2000 (Act 573)).' The *Diamonds Act, 1972 (N.R.C.D. 32)* has similar provisions which are found in its section 13 entitled '*Alien offender liable to deportation*' and reads: 'Where an alien is convicted of an offence under this Act, the alien is, after paying the fine or serving the sentence, liable to deportation under section 36 of the *Immigration Act, 2000 (Act 573)*.'

45. The *Refugee Law of 1992(P.N.D.C.L. 305D)* and the establishment of a Refugee Board in 1993 pursuant to that law have streamlined issues regarding the granting of refugee status in accordance with Ghana's obligations under international laws, conventions and protocols. *P.N.D.C.L. 305D* has five main parts: (i) *Prohibition of Expulsion of Refugees*; (ii) *Establishment of the Refugee Board*; (iii) *Procedure for Application and Grant of Refugee Status, Appeals,* etc.; (iv) *Rights and Duties of Refugees*; and (v) *Miscellaneous matters*, that includes a list of the articles in the *United Nations Convention relating to the Status of Refugees of 1951; the Protocol Relating to the Status of Refugees of 1967*; and the Organisation of African Unity (OAU)*Convention Governing the Specific Aspects of Refugee Problems in Africa.*

46. The *Human Trafficking Act, 2005 (Act 694)* provides detailed rules to prevent, combat and punish the trafficking in persons. Several other laws regulate immigration and related issues. These include the *1992 Constitution*, Chapter 5 of which safeguards fundamental human rights and freedoms including the right of movement, the right of entry into Ghana, the right to personal liberty and the right to dignity of the person. It also prohibits torture, inhuman or degrading treatment, slavery, servitude and forced labour. The *Criminal Offences Act, 1960 (Act 29)* has similar provisions in its sections 71 (exposing a child to danger), 97 (rape), 101 (defilement), 107 (procuration), 273 (allowing persons under age to be in brothels) and 314 (slave dealing). Section 46 of the *Children's Act, 1998 (Act 560)* deals with unlawful child removal and section 58 of the *Labour Act, 2000* (651) and Regulation 7 of the *Labour Regulations, 2007 (L.I.1833)* prohibit employment of young persons in hazardous work, etc.

III. Judicial and Administrative Authorities in Ghana

47. This section offers a brief introductory description of the judicial and administrative institutional framework for the resolution of migration disputes in Ghana.

A. *The Judicial System*

48. Ghana has a multi-layered, hierarchical judiciary. It comprises two sets of courts: the superior court of judicature and the lower courts of judicature. The former group consists of the Supreme Court, the Court of Appeal and the High Court Regional Tribunals in descending order of authority. These Courts are expressly established by the Constitution[7] and are, therefore, fundamental to dispute resolution in Ghana. The second group, i.e., the lower courts of judicature are established under the authority of the Constitution though not expressly.[8] The lower courts in Ghana are: the circuit courts, the district courts, the national and regional houses of chiefs and all traditional councils.

The Supreme Court

49. The Supreme Court is the highest court of the country.[9] It has no branches and is presently situated in the capital city, Accra, although it may be relocated to any place indicated by the Chief Justice.[10] It comprises the Chief Justice and at least nine justices.[11] Its quorum is five Justices of the Supreme Court,[12] but in interlocutory matters one judge may make a ruling which on appeal will be heard by a panel of three Justices.[13]

The Supreme Court is the final appellate court[14] and only has original jurisdiction in matters of constitutional interpretation and judicial review of legislation.[15] Thus, this Court does not serve as a Court of First Instance with respect to migration issues, unless the issues pertain to constitutional interpretation or the judicial review of legislation. Its decisions cannot be appealed, but the Court may review its own decisions.[16] Grounds for such review are: exceptional circumstances which have led to a miscarriage of justice; evidence that was not available at the time of the last decision.[17]

50. The Supreme Court supervises all other courts through the issue of prerogative writs.[18] It may hear and decide a petition for the exercise of the president's prerogative of mercy at his request or merely advise him on such.[19] It has the power to affirm or quash a conviction and increase or decrease a sentence within the range

7. Refer to Arts 128 (1), 136 (1), 139(1), and 142(1) of the 1992 fourth republican Constitution of the Republic of Ghana.
8. *See* Art. 126(1)(b) of the 1992 fourth republican Constitution of the Republic of Ghana.
9. Constitution, Art. 129(1–4).
10. Section 38 of *Act 459* as amended by *Act 620*, subject to Art. 136, cl. 4.
11. Section 1(1)of the Courts Act, 1993, Act 459.
12. Section 1(2) of the Courts Act, 1993, Act 459.
13. Section of the Courts Act, 1993, Act 459.
14. Article 129(1) of the 1992 Constitution;, s. 2(1). of the Courts Act, 1993, Act 459.
15. Article 130 of the 1992 Constitution; s. 3 of the Courts Act, 1993, Act 459.
16. Section 6 of the Courts Act, 1993, Act 459.
17. Rule 54, Supreme Court Rules CI16.
18. Section 5 of the Courts Act, 1993, Act 459.
19. Section 9 of the Courts Act, 1993, Act 459.

that the Court of First Instance had the power to convict.[20] A migrant who has been convicted and sentenced may appeal either his conviction or sentence or both to the Supreme Court as the final appellate Court.

Court of Appeal.

51. The Court of Appeal is the second court in the hierarchy of courts. It consists of the Chief Justice and at least ten justices of the Court but has a quorum of three justices.[21] It has jurisdiction to hear appeals in all cases decided by the High Court or Regional Tribunals and in all civil and interlocutory criminal matters decided by the Circuit Court.[22] Thus, a migrant may appeal an unfavourable decision, including, but not limited to the revocation or renewal of his or her permit to the Court of Appeal. While some appeals are always permitted under law, others require leave of the court whose decision is being appealed and in some cases, the Court of Appeal itself.[23] It has the power to affirm or quash a conviction and increase or decrease a sentence within the range that the Court of First Instance had the power to convict.[24] A single Justice of the Court of Appeal may rule on an interlocutory matter and his decision may be appealed before a panel of three justices of the Court of Appeal.

High Court

52. The High Court consists of the Chief Justice and at least twenty justices.[25] The High Court has the broadest jurisdiction of all the courts allowing it to hear cases concerning the following matters in the following ways: (i) original jurisdiction in all matters, (ii) appellate criminal jurisdiction from Circuit Court, (iii) appellate jurisdiction in all decisions of the District and Juvenile Courts and (iv) Fundamental Human Rights enforcement jurisdiction.[26] It also has exclusive jurisdiction in piracy matters[27] and maritime disputes[28] and protective jurisdiction over infants[29]and incompetents.[30] The latter makes it the proper forum for all matters relating to the custody of infants and incompetents. Finally, it has supervisory jurisdiction over lower courts. Thus, a migrant may seek to enforce his or her rights under Article 33 of the 1992 constitution by making an application to the High Court to have same enforced. Similarly, migrants, in their interactions with administrative bodies such as the Immigration service, GIPC and the Free Zones Board, may under Article 23 of the 1992 constitution seek redress at the High Court or any

20. Section 33(9) of the Courts Act, 1993, Act 459.
21. Section 10 of the Courts Act, 1993, Act 459.
22. Section 11 of the Courts Act, 1993, Act 459.
23. Section 11(5) of the Courts Act, 1993, Act 459.
24. Section 33(9) of the Courts Act, 1993, Act 459.
25. Section 14(1) of the Courts Act, 1993, Act 459.
26. Section 15 of the Courts Act, 1993, Act 459.
27. Section 17 of the Courts Act, 1993, Act 459.
28. Section 20 of the Courts Act, 1993, Act 459.
29. Section 18 of the Courts Act, 1993, Act 459.
30. Section 19 of the Courts Act, 1993, Act 459.

court or tribunal for that matter.[31] The High Court has a quorum of one justice unless the charge is treason or high treason in which case three justices are required.[32] It may hear criminal cases either alone or with the aid of a jury or with the aid of assessors.[33] The High Court has different divisions which may be added as needed.[34] At present the divisions are the Commercial, Land and Family Divisions. It has the power to affirm or quash a conviction and increase or decrease a sentence within the range that the Court of First Instance had the power to convict.[35]

Regional Tribunals

53. These Regional Tribunals were originally established by the PNDC/AFRC military regime to specifically try offences against the State. They are the only non-traditional judicial courts that were absorbed into the traditional judiciary system under the authority of the Constitution.[36] It has concurrent status with the High Court, and its chairman must be qualified to sit as a High Court Judge.[37] It consists of a Chief Justice, chairperson and a panel of as many persons as the Chief Justice should decide necessary.[38] It has jurisdiction in criminal matters, particularly in relation to the *Special Offences of Act 29*, such as narcotics related offences, customs related offences and serious economic fraud or loss to the State. A migrant may be tried by a Regional Tribunal for these stated offences.[39] Appeals from its decisions are made to the Court of Appeal.[40] The superior courts have the power to commit for contempt.[41] Their justices are required to be of high moral character and have legal experience. They may sit at any place, as determined by the Chief Justice.[42]

Lower Courts: Circuit Court

54. At present there are two groups of lower courts: the conventional State Courts, i.e.,(a) Circuit Courts, (b) District courts and (c) Juvenile courts, (in descending order of hierarchy), on the one hand, and the National House of Chiefs, Regional Houses of Chiefs and Traditional councils (in descending order of authority),[43] on the other hand. Other lower courts may be established as and when the Chief Justice finds this is necessary.[44] The Circuit Court is empowered to try all civil

31. Section 16 of the Courts Act, 1993, Act 459.
32. Section 14(2) of the Courts Act, 1993, Act 459.
33. Section 14(2) of the Courts Act, 1993, Act 459.
34. Section 14(3) of the Courts Act, 1993, Act 459.
35. Section 33(9) of the Courts Act, 1993, Act 459.
36. Article 142(1) of the 1992 Constitution.
37. Section 14(2) of the Courts Act, 1993, Act 459.
38. Section 23 of the Courts Act, 1993, Act 459.
39. Section 24 of the Courts Act, 1993, Act 459.
40. Section 25 of the Courts Act, 1993, Act 459.
41. Section 36 of the Courts Act, 1993, Act 459.
42. Section 38 of the Courts Act, 1993, Act 459.
43. Section 39 of the Courts Act, 1993, Act 459.
44. Section 39(e) of the Courts Act, 1993, Act 459.

matters[45] and all criminal matters with the exception of capital offences, treason and indictable offences.[46] The Circuit Court can adjudicate on matters within its jurisdiction or competence involving migrants. Civil appeals from circuit court decisions are made to the Court of Appeal while criminal appeals are made to the High Court.[47]

District and Juvenile Courts

55. There are as many District and Juvenile Courts in any district as the Chief Justice chooses.[48] Each court has its own designated area of jurisdiction.[49] Its magistrates do not need to be lawyers.[50] A District and Juvenile Court can have civil[51] and criminal jurisdiction. Criminal jurisdiction is, however, limited to offences triable summarily and or which carry a maximum punishment of either 500 penalty units, two years imprisonment or both.[52]

The Chief Justice may designate any District Court as a Juvenile Court.[53] This gives it the authority to try offences committed by minors as well as offences under the *Children's Act*.[54] The District and Juvenile Courts can adjudicate on matters within their competence involving migrants. To minimize instances of injustice occasioned by errors/incompetence of District Courts, magistrates are required to send a monthly list of all criminal cases handled by them and the outcome of these cases to its supervising High Court Judge who may, upon study of the record, reverse or modify the sentence.[55]

B. Administrative Institutions or Authorities in Ghana

Ghana Immigration Service

56. The *Immigration Service Law, 1989 (PNDCL 226)* establishes the *GIS* to administer all issues related to immigration in Ghana. The *Immigration Act 2000 (Act 573)* also lays down rules that immigration officers use to admit or refuse entry to persons seeking permission to enter Ghana. The *GIS* regulates and monitors the movements and activities of foreigners in Ghana. Various provisions in Ghana's *1992 Constitution* require administrative officers, such as immigration officials and persons or authorities vested with discretionary power, to be fair and candid, and to exercise their discretionary power in a way that is not arbitrary, capricious, or biased

45. Section 42 of the Courts Act, 1993, Act 459.
46. Section 43 of the Courts Act, 1993, Act 459.
47. Section 44 of the Courts Act, 1993, Act 459.
48. Section 45(1) of the Courts Act, 1993, Act 459.
49. Section 45(2) of the Courts Act, 1993, Act 459.
50. Sections 45(2) and 46(1) of the Courts Act, 1993, Act 459.
51. Section 47 of the Courts Act, 1993, Act 459.
52. Section 48 of the Courts Act, 1993, Act 459.
53. Section (49(1) of the Courts Act, 1993, Act 459.
54. Section 50 of the Courts Act, 1993, Act 459.
55. Section 52 of the Courts Act, 1993, Act 459.

either by resentment, prejudice or personal dislike, but in accordance with due process of law and published regulations (Article 296). Moreover, as noted *supra*, Article 23 of the 1992 Constitution provides that 'administrative bodies and administrative officials shall act fairly and reasonably and comply with the requirements imposed on them by law, and persons aggrieved by the exercise of such acts and decisions shall have the right to seek redress before a court or other tribunal'. Article 33 also permits a party aggrieved by human rights violation to make an application to the High Court, with a right of appeal to the Court of Appeal and further to the Supreme Court.

57. The Immigration Service also serves as a front line agency, which ensures that the vision of Ghana becoming the gateway to Africa is achieved. This is done through several activities, including: examination of travellers entering or leaving Ghana, examination of application forms of foreign nationals applying for extension or variation of existing permits and examination of applications for visa, entry permits and permits for entering prohibited areas, and authorization of such visas and permits in appropriate cases.

58. GIS also controls foreign nationals in Ghana, their employment and movements, and ensures compliance with immigration laws and regulations. They ensure that unnecessary restrictions are not placed in the way of foreign nationals wishing to enter or remain as investors and give advice about the immigration laws and regulations to people wishing to enter, remain in or leave Ghana. They are also empowered to investigate breaches of the immigration laws and regulation, and conduct court prosecution of foreign nationals who are in Ghana without permits. GIS also processes passport applications in the districts and the regions, and liaise with other agencies with responsibilities for security, the combating of crime and other issues relating to the public good in the performance of their functions.

59. The immigration laws of Ghana provide several procedural safeguards. Section 7(1) and 7(2) of *Act 573* provide that 'where an immigration officer is in doubt as to the right of a person to enter Ghana, the officer may send that person to be detained, and that person shall remain in custody pending the determination of the matter'. 'The Director may, pending the completion of enquiries in respect of a detained person, release that person from custody on the directions determined by the Director and may for that purpose issue a temporary permit to that person.' If a person is deemed a prohibited immigrant, he is still given an opportunity to rebut the presumption, but the burden of proof that he is not a prohibited immigrant lies on him, according to section 8(3) of *Act 573*.

60. Section 19(1) of Act 573 entitled '*High Court may revoke the right of abode status*' provides that the High Court may on an application by the Attorney-General, deprive a person with a right of abode status of that status when, (a)the activities of that person are inimical to the security of the State or prejudicial to public order, public health, morality or public interest; (b) the right was acquired by fraudulent misrepresentation or any other illegal or irregular means; or (c) the holder of the status no longer qualifies under the Act. Thus even where the Director of Immigration seeks to revoke the permit of a person on grounds of fraudulent misrepresentation, concealment, or any other illegal practice, or on grounds that the conditions governing the permit have been broken, or merely to impose fresh conditions in relation to that permit, the Director has to use the process in section 19(1) as stated *supra*. Moreover, the Director has to take reasonable steps to communicate notice of the revocation, or other new conditions, to the person concerned. The revocation notice is usually given in accordance with *Form K* of the *Immigration Regulations*, 2001 (L.I.1691). Such notification is required under section 19(3) and, under section 19(5), it is also a notification to a person whose name is endorsed in the permit, a spouse of the holder of the permit where the spouse was issued the permit as a consequence of the issuing of a permit to the other spouse, and a dependant of the holder of the permit who is not a citizen.

61. Several other procedural safeguards are applicable in such matters. A petitioner has a constitutional right under Article 19 of the 1992 constitution to be represented by a lawyer of his choice. Moreover, although a petition to the Minister under section 46 does not stay the action which has been petitioned against, the petitioner may be permitted to stay in Ghana pending the hearing of the petition made by him (section 47). Section 51 empowers the Minister to revoke or *waive* a visa, permit, condition of entry and any other requirement on grounds of national interest, compassionate circumstances or any other reasonable ground. All these procedural rules plus the right to petition the Minister under section 46 assure very good procedural safeguards in immigration matters in Ghana.

The Ghana Refugee Board

62. The Ghana Refugee Board (GRB) was set up in 1993 pursuant to *Refugee Law, 1992 (PNDCL 305D)* to streamline issues on the grant of refugee status in Ghana in accordance with Ghana's obligations under international laws, conventions and protocols. The GRB deals with Refugee Status Determination and communicates a decision to the asylum seeker in writing as to whether his/her claim as a refugee has been accepted or refused. An asylum seeker can appeal against an adverse decision within thirty days upon receiving the decision. The Director of Immigration, upon recommendation of the Refugee Board, shall issue any relevant immigrant document to a refugee present in Ghana. Where the Board is of the opinion that a refugee should not have been accorded refugee status or no longer qualifies as a refugee, they may withdraw that person's refugee status and notify the refugee in writing.

The GIPC

63. The GIPC was established pursuant to the *Ghana Investment Promotion Centre Act, 2013 (Act 865)* to encourage investment in Ghana by providing a clear and stable institutional framework for investors. The GIPC provides key services to investors on immigration issues especially in the field of employment. It advises and registers investors, monitors and enforces the exclusion of foreigners from business operations that are exclusively reserved for Ghanaians, administers and enforces the foreign capital requirements for enterprises in which foreign participation is permitted, and facilitates the immigrant quota allocation arrangements for foreign investors. An enterprise that intends to employ an expatriate applies to the GIPC for facilitation of the employment. Such application shall specify the number of expatriates to be employed; and the application so submitted shall be dealt with by the GIS in consultation with the GIPC.

The Ghana Free Zones Board

64. The Ghana Free Zones Board (GFZB) was established by the *Ghana Free Zones Act, 1995 (Act 504)* as amended by the *Free Zone (Amendment) Act, 2002 (Act 618)* to provide for the establishment of free zones to aid economic development by creating an attractive and conducive business environment through the provision of competitive free zone incentives. The Board regulates activities in these free zones. It focuses on promoting investment in especially the manufacturing sector with the aim of exporting the bulk of the products and provides for the participation of foreign investors in the Free Zones. A person is not permitted to carry on a trade, business or industry within a free zone unless, among other requirements, he or she is registered and the GFZB has given him an incorporated licence authorizing the carrying on of that trade, business or industry. The GFZB provides information and investment opportunities in the free zone, assists enterprises in securing other permits from related Agencies such as the Immigration Service, the Environmental Protection Agency, the Ghana Water Company, the Electricity Company. It also provides serviced land and utilities facilities in the designated export processing zones, and other services requested by investors.

The Commission on Human Rights and Administrative Justice

65. The Commission was established in 1993, by the *Commission on Human Rights and Administrative Justice Act (Act 456)*, in accordance with Article 216 of the 1992 Constitution, as an independent agency charged with safeguarding human rights in Ghana. Its purpose is to provide people who do not have access to the regular courts, for instance due to financial constraints, with protection by the state. Thus unlike the regular courts which only hear the parties, Commission on Human Rights and Administrative Justice(CHRAJ) can take proactive steps to investigate the complaint with or without the cooperation of the accused party. It has a chairperson and two deputies who are qualified to be appointed as a judge for the Court of Appeal and High Court, respectively.[56] CHRAJ investigates complaints of the following nature: (a) abuse of office, unfair treatment, injustice or violation of human rights by a public official operating in his official capacity; (b) the administrative workings of state institutions; and (c) violations of constitutional rights by any person.[57] It has jurisdiction to deal with such matters within their competence relating to migrants. The Commission is responsible for resolving problems through such means as are fair, proper and effective, including (i) negotiation and seeking a com

---

56. Section 3(1) *The Commission on Human Rights and Administrative Justice Act (Act 456).*
57. Section 7.

promise between the parties concerned; (ii) ensuring that the complaint and its finding on it are reported to the superior of an offending person; (iii) bringing proceedings in a competent court for a remedy to secure the termination of the offending action or conduct, or the abandonment or alteration of the offending procedures. It is also empowered to take action to resolve the conflict based on its findings.[58] To prevent jurisdictional overlap and undue manipulation, its jurisdiction is limited to matters which are not dealt with before the courts. It has no jurisdiction on international affairs or presidential pardons.[59] It is not compelled to investigate every complaint. It may declare a complaint trivial,[60] or direct the complainant to other, readily available, remedies.

Challenges

66. A complaint must be put to the CHRAJ in writing and signed or thumb printed before it comes before the Commission.[61] Thus, complainants are limited to those who are either literate or in a position to contract a literate person to write his complaint. Due to financial constraints only eighty-nine district offices have been established and staffed. They have limited powers of enforcement, for instance, lack of power to prosecute corruption cases or fine or commit for contempt other than for failure to honour a subpoena. They have no statutory power to verify the accuracy of the Assets Declaration Forms submitted to the Auditor-General. They are funded by centralized funding system.[62] There may be problems due to the fact that funds are not being released promptly.

67. Although under section 15(2) of *Act 456*, the CHRAJ can summon before it and examine on oath or affirmation – a person required to give information or produce anything, document or paper, a complainant or any person who the CHRAJ considers will be able to give information – it cannot, under section 15(3) and (4) of that Act, compel a person to give evidence or produce papers or documents if that person is bound by law to maintain secrecy in relation to, or not to disclose, any matter, if compliance with that requirement would be in breach of the obligation of secrecy or non-disclosure.

National Labour Commission

68. The National Labour Commission of Ghana is established under the *Labour Act, Act 651.*[63] Its purpose is to receive and deal with industrial disputes and promote relations between labour and management.[64] It has jurisdiction to deal with matters within their competence affecting or relating to migrants. When settling disputes, the Commission has the same powers as the High Court to enforce atten

58. Section 9.
59. Section 8(2).
60. Section 13(1)-(2).
61. Section 12 (1)-(3).
62. (Consolidated Fund) Section 21.
63. (Section 135) *Labour Act.*
64. Section 138(1).

dance and examine witnesses and require the production of documents.[65] In respect of its proceedings, the privileges and immunities enjoyed by the Commission are the same as those of the High Court.[66] Under the *Labour Act, (Act 651)* parties involved in industrial disputes must first negotiate in good faith per the terms in the collective agreement or the contract of employment.[67] If this process fails within seven days of the start of the dispute, either party or both parties may request the assistance of the Commission for the appointment of a mediator.[68] The Commission can also order, within a period determined at their discretion, that the parties in dispute comply with the procedures stipulated in the collective agreement, where the parties have either not exhausted these procedures or have not agreed to waive them.[69] If negotiations fail, the parties have three days within which to conclude the mediation process.[70] The parties are given the chance to choose their mediator(s), who shall then be appointed by the Commission. The mediation must be concluded within a period of fourteen days, and if, at the end of this time, a settlement has been reached, the terms of the settlement are recorded and deemed to be binding on both parties.[71] The parties may opt for voluntary arbitration if mediation fails.[72] The decision of the arbitrator is binding on the parties.[73] The parties can agree to the method of selecting an arbitrator empanelling a panel to arbitrate the matter, or, in the absence of such agreement, the Commission appoints an arbitrator panel.[74]

If a dispute remains unresolved after a lock out or a strike, the Commission may settle the dispute by compulsory arbitration.[75] The parties are served a notice in which the Commission states what the issues appear to be, and requesting the parties to either agree or disagree with the stated issues.[76] The matter should be settled within fourteen days of service of the notice[77] by a three member arbitration panel, one each from the government, Organized Labour and the Employers' Organization.[78] The award must be published in the gazette and other state media.[79] Where a party is unsatisfied by the award at the end of the arbitration, the party may appeal to the Court of Appeal, on questions of law within seven days after the publication of the award.[80]

Challenges

65. Section 139(2).
66. Section 139(3).
67. Section 153.
68. Section 154.
69. Section 154(2).
70. Section 154(3).
71. Section 154(4)-(5).
72. Section 157.
73. Section 158.
74. Section 156.
75. Section 160.
76. Section 164(1).
77. Section 164(2).
78. Section 164(3).
79. Section 167(1).
80. Section 167(2).

69. The complaint should be written and submitted to the Commission. While this does not necessarily exclude, it does increase the inconvenience involved for the large unions within the informal sectors.

Domestic Violence and Victim Support Unit (DOVVSU)

70. The Domestic Violence and Victim Support Unit is a specialized unit of the Ghana Police Service, charged with addressing the increased cases of abuse and violence against women and children, and men where necessary, as well as with researching the characteristics and trends of crimes against women and children, and was first established as Women and Juvenile Unit (WAJU) in 1998 but was eventually transformed into DOVVSU in 2005. The functions of DOVVSU include investigating all female and child related offences; handling cases involving domestic violence, child abuse, juvenile offences, child delinquency; and arresting and prosecuting all such cases, where necessary. DOVVSU deals with cases involving migrants in relation to such matters. The role of DOVVSU within the Ghana Police Service also includes protecting the rights of the vulnerable against all forms of abuse; establishing an effective database for crime detection, prevention and prosecution; collaborating with organizations that may be able to offer assistance to victims in need of assistance (shelter, medical, legal, etc.), and with other organizations that may be able to offer specialized help i.e., referrals (medical, clinical psychological support, etc.); and investigating all cases of domestic violence and child abuse.

71. The forms of abuse most often reported to the unit run the gamut from physical to socio-economic. The unit also deals with a wide range of sexual offences including rape, defilement, sodomy and criminal abortion. Other offences dealt with by DOVVSU are categorized as child related offences like abduction, child trafficking, and exposing a child to harm, non-maintenance, child abandonment, etc. with the exception of serious sexual offences, child related cases, and matters involving serious assault, all other cases are prosecuted only after the complainant has given consent.

Economic and Organised Crime Office

72. This agency was set up by *Act 804* of 2010, in accordance with Article 190(1)(d) of the *1992 Constitution*, in pursuance of the State's anti-corruption agenda. It is a specialized agency of government to monitor, investigate and, on the authority of the Attorney-General, prosecute any offence involving serious financial and economic loss to the State and to make provision for connected and incidental purposes. It can investigate and prosecute migrants on such matters. The Economic and Organised Crime Office(EOCO) has a seven member Governing Board which has the general control of the Office on matters of policy. The overall administration and operation of the office falls under the direction of the Executive Director. Through regular, reliability checks of management practices applied by public institutions, effective economic crime prevention and public awareness programmes, and the investigation and prosecution of offenders, the EOCO aims to strengthen public accountability in the utilization and management of the State's financial and economic resources to the general benefit of Ghana.

The EOCO employs strategically, techniques of prevention and detection. The former encompasses policies, procedures, training, and communication that prevent the occurrence of fraud, while the latter relates to activities and skills that discover in a timely manner, that fraud has occurred or is occurring. The mandate to investigate any suspected fraud is inherent to the Office and can be activated by the Executive Director without reference to any other authority or agency of the State.[81]

Family Tribunals

73. The Family Tribunal system is composed of various institutions, including family tribunal courts, the Ministry of Women and Children's Affairs, the Child Panel, the Department of Social Welfare, the foster care system, SOS villages, children's homes and orphanages, the socio-legal centre of Defence for Children International (DCI), and specialized probation officers and social workers. The formal system set up to protect the rights of children, was founded on the *Children's Act 1998 as amended.*[82] Family Tribunals are panels composed of a chairperson and between two and four other panel members, which include a social welfare officer.[83] Family Tribunals have jurisdiction in matters concerning parentage, custody, and access to and maintenance of children.[84] It can deal with cases involving migrants in relation to such matters. Only the members and officers of a Family Tribunal, the parties concerned in the matter, the parent guardian of the child, probation and social welfare officers and other authorized persons are allowed to attend a sitting of the tribunal.[85] A child has the right to participate in any decision which affects his well-being.[86] Proceedings in a Family Tribunal are informal and conducted by enquiry.[87]

74. When the Department of Social Welfare receives a report of child abuse or endangerment and it is determined that the child is not in immediate danger, the matter is referred to a Child Panel, a non-judicial board charged with mediating matters concerning children. If the investigation by the Department shows that the child has been abused or is in immediate need of care and protection, the *Children's Act* authorizes the removal of the child to a place of safety.[88] When a child is removed, the child must be brought before a Family Tribunal within seven days.[89] The Family Tribunal can then make a care order to determine the placement of the child or a supervision order setting out the terms under which a child may remain in the cus

81. Section 3(1)(a)-(d) and (2); ss 12 and 13.
82. Section 33(1); *see also* Children's (Amendment) Act, 2016 (Act 937).
83. Section 34.
84. Section 35.
85. Section 36(1).
86. Section 30.
87. Section 37.
88. Section 19(3).
89. Section 19(4).

tody of his parent(s), guardian(s), or relative(s).[90] The rights of the child at a Family Tribunal include *inter alia*, 'a right to legal representation', 'a right to give an account, and express an opinion at a Family Tribunal', and the right to appeal.[91]

§3. Overview of International Legal Instruments Applicable in Ghana

75. Many international legal instruments on migration are applicable in Ghana. However, since there is no comprehensive international treaty regulating all aspects of international migration, the relevant applicable international laws deal with specific issues on migration such as refugees, trafficking, rights of migrant workers, free movement of persons, goods, services, and capital, and to the right of residence and establishment, etc. These include:

(1) *The 1951 UN Convention Relating to the Status of Refugees* (Geneva, 28 July 1951, entered into force on 22 April 1954) (*see* section 11 and Schedule of *Refugee Law, 1992 (P.N.D.C.L. 305D)*).
(2) *The 1967 UN Protocol Relating to the Status of Refugees* (31 January 1967, entered into force on 4 October 1967) (*see* section 11 and Schedule of *Refugee Law, 1992 (P.N.D.C.L. 305D)*).
(3) *OAU (now AU) Convention Governing the Specific Aspects of Refugee Problems in Africa* (Adopted by the Assembly of Heads of State and Government at its Sixth Ordinary Session in Addis Ababa on 10 September 1969, it entered into force on 20 June 1974) (*see* section 11 and Schedule of *Refugee Law, 1992 (P.N.D.C.L. 305D)*).
(4) *The ECOWAS Treaty of 1975.*
(5) *The Revised ECOWAS Treaty of 1997.*
(6) *The 1979 Protocol on the Free Movement of Persons, Right of Residence and Establishment (*Protocol A/P1/5/79*)*:
  (a) *The 1982 Protocol on the Definition of Community Citizenship* (Protocol A/P3/5/82).
  (b) *The 1984 Resolution of the Authority of Heads of State and Government on the First Phase of the Protocol on Free Movement of Persons, the Right of Residence and Establishment* (A/RES.2/11/84).
  (c) *The 1985 Supplementary Protocol on the Code of Conduct for the Implementation of the Protocol on Free Movement of Persons, the Right of Residence and Establishment* (A/SP1/7/85).
  (d) *The 1986 Supplementary Protocol on the Second Phase (right of residence) of the Protocol on Free Movement of Persons, the Right of Residence and Establishment* (A/SP1/7/86).
  (e) *The 1989 Supplementary Protocol amending and complementing provisions of Article 7 of the Protocol on Free Movement of Persons, the Right of Residence and Establishment* (A/SP1/6/89).

90. Section 20(1).
91. Section 38.

(f) *The 1990 Supplementary Protocol on the implementation of the Third Phase (right of establishment) of the Protocol on Free Movement of Persons, the Right of Residence and Establishment* (A/SP2/5/90).
(g) *The 1982 Decision amending the provisions of Article 27 of the Treaty of ECOWAS* (A/DEC.8/5/82).
(h) *The 1982 Decision on the Application of the Protocol on the Free Movement of Persons and the Public Enlightenment Programme* (A/DEC.210/5/82).
(i) *The 1985 Decision of the Authority of Heads of State and Government relating to the Establishment of ECOWAS Travel Certificate for Member States* (A/DEC.2/7/85).
(j) *The 1990 Decision establishing a Residence Card in ECOWAS Member States* (A/DEC.2/5/90).

(7) *African Charter on Human and Peoples Rights* (adopted on 27 June 1981 in Banjul, the Gambia, and entered into force on 21 October 1986).
(8) *The 1990 Convention on the Rights of Migrant Workers and Members of their Families* (Adopted by the General Assembly at its 45th Session on 18 December 1990 (A/RES/45/158). The Convention came into force on 1 July 2003, following the ratification by twenty countries).
(9) *The 1949 Convention (No. 97 and Recommendation No. 86) concerning Migration for Employment.*
(10) *The 1975 Convention (No. 143 and Recommendation No. 151) concerning Migration in Abusive Conditions and the Promotion of Equality of Opportunity and Treatment of Migrant Workers.*
(11) *The 2002 Protocol against the Smuggling of Migrants by Land, Sea and Air* (supplementing the 2000 United Nationals Convention against Transnational Organized Crime).
(12) *The 2002 Protocol to Prevent, Suppress and Punish Trafficking in Persons, especially Women and Children* (supplementing the 2000 United Nationals Convention against Transnational Organized Crime).
(13) *The 1948 United Nations Universal Declaration of Human Rights* (UDHR):
(a) *International Covenant on Civil and Political Rights* (ICCPR).
(b) *International Covenant on Economic, Social and Cultural Rights* (ICESCR).
(14) *The Declaration on the Human Rights of Individuals who are not Nationals of the country in which they Live* (adopted by the UN Gen. Ass. in 1985).
(15) *Programme of Action of the United Nations Conference on Population and Development, Chapter 10.*
(16) *The 1986 United Nations Declaration on the Right to Development (*Adopted by the General Assembly of the United Nations, Resolution 41/128 of 4 December 1986*).*
(17) *The Fourth Geneva Convention on the Protection of Civilian Persons in Time of War of 12 August 1949 and its Protocols* (came into force on 7 December 1978).
(18) *The United Nations Human Rights Committee 1999 General Comment 27 on 'Freedom of Movement'.*

Part I. Border Control and Entrance

Chapter 1. Organization of Border Control

76. Natural persons, vehicles, cargoes and goods crossing the country's border are subject to border, customs and other types of control provided for under various national legislations, at the designated entry-exit points. Having evolved into a highly stable country politically and economically with a commitment to constitutional democracy and free enterprise, Ghana has put in place many border control systems. However, Ghana still lacks adequate personnel, equipment and it also has some porous borders that pose migration control challenges. This is not entirely surprising in a country where national construction only commenced in the late 1950s and throughout the 1960s following independence.

77. The control of borders for purposes of migration lies with the GIS and other border control agencies, for example the Ghana Customs Excise and Preventive Service (CEPS), border guards, Plant Protection and Regulatory Services, Public Health Officers, Veterinary Officers. The Border Patrol Unit of the GIS was officially inaugurated at the GIS headquarters on 1 November 2006 by the then Interior Minister Mr Kan Dapaah. The Unit had a workforce of about 800 agents at the end of 2008. The objective of the Unit is to ensure the security of all borders, entry and exit points including coastal areas against illegal entry and exit by cross-border criminals. In the performance of their responsibilities, the Immigration Service Border Patrol Unit undertakes tasks such as the physical patrolling of the borders, checking for illegal migration, drug/human trafficking, smuggling across the border and animal trafficking and the reporting on all forms of suspected subversive activities. It must also be prepared to act as the first line of defence against external aggressors for the Ghana Armed Forces.

78. Section 2 of the *Immigration Act, 2000, (Act 573)* provides that a person entering Ghana shall enter at an authorized point and shall proceed to the nearest immigration office, produce his travel document and complete the prescribed forms. A person who arrives by sea or air in Ghana at a place other than an authorized place or port shall, within forty-eight hours, proceed and report to the immigration officer at the nearest immigration post. An immigration officer to whom a person reports, shall, if the person is not prohibited from entering Ghana, and he is satisfied by documentary or other evidence of the person's identity, grant that person entry permission. According to section 3 of the *Immigration Act, 2000, (Act 573)*, headed '*Illegal Place of Entry and Border Resident*', a person shall not enter Ghana except by one of the approved places of entry. That section explains an approved place of entry to be a place in Ghana in respect of which landing or docking rights have been granted to an aircraft or vessel or a place specified in the Schedule to the Act. Table 13 shows the places specified in the Schedule of *Act 573* grouped under the regions of Ghana.

Table 13 Approved Places of Entry into Ghana

GREATER ACCRA REGION	*NORTHERN REGION*	*UPPER WEST REGION*
(1) Kotoka International Airport	(1) Bole-Chache	(1) Hamile
(2) Tema	(2) Tatale	(2) Tumu

UPPER EAST REGION	(1)Bawku-Missiga	(2)Kulungugu	(3)Mognori	(4)Namoo	(5)Paga	(6)Pulimankon
BRONG-AHAFO REGION	(1)Atuna	(2) Dormaa Ahenkro-Gonokrom	(3)Nkrankwanta	(4)Kofibadukrom	(5)Kwameseikrom	(6)Sampa

WESTERN REGION	1. Ellanda Wharf	2. Dadieso	3. Elubo	4. Half Assini	5. Newtown
	6. Jaway Wharf	7. Oseikojokrom	8. Sewum	9. Takoradi Harbour	10. Yaakese

VOLTA REGION	1. Aflao	2. Akanu	3. Baglo	4. Batume	5. Have-Avi
	6. Honuta	7. Kpoglo	8. Leklebi Dafor	9. Leklebi Kame	10.Menusu
	11. Nyive	12.Shia	13.Tinjase	14.Wli Afegame	15.Yawgu

79. Section 3(4) of *Act 573* states that regulations may be drawn up under this Act to provide for free movement across the border of a border-resident for the purpose of attending to his or her routine economic or social matters. A *border-resident* is defined by the interpretation section 56 of *Act 573* to mean a national of a neighbouring country who ordinarily resides within a 5 kilometre radius of either side of Ghana's territorial frontiers with the Republics of Togo, Burkina Faso and Cote d'Ivoire. Section 3(5) of *Act 573* states that anyone who violates the law and enters

Ghana through an unapproved route commits an offence and is liable, on summary conviction, to a fine or imprisonment for a term not exceeding twelve months or to both.

80. The Ghana Customs Excise and Preventive Service (CEPS) also plays a critical role in border control. The main focus of CEPS is on revenue collection and the movement of goods across national borders, yet, as its name indicates, but it also plays an important role in many other areas of border control and addresses security concerns. Charged with policing the nation's borders and regulating the movement of people and goods in and out of Ghana under the *Customs, Excise and Preventive Service (Management) Law, 1993 (PNDCL 330)*, CEPS is the most powerful front-line agency in Ghana's border zones including land frontiers, the harbour, airport, and the virtual space of electronic networks. As the first line of defence at the nation's entry points, CEPS occupies a unique position in border control and its officers bear arms, making it a Paramilitary institution. The preventive functions of CEPS thus make it responsible for indirectly regulating the movement of people at the country's borders.

81. There are several Ghanaian laws on national border controls that have an impact on migration. These laws include the *Quarantine Ordinance (1951) (Cap 77)* which makes provision for preventing the introduction of disease into Ghana, or any part thereof, from an infected place. It also seeks to prevent the transmission of diseases from Ghana into any other country. The *Infectious Diseases Ordinance (1951) (Cap 78)* seeks to prevent the spread of infectious and contagious diseases. Other relevant legislation are the *Public Order Act, 1994 (Act 491)*, and the *Environmental Protection Agency Act, 1994 (Act 490)*. Thus, the institutions responsible for the implementation of these laws are usually involved in border control activities. These include the Plant Protection and Regulatory Services, Public Health Officers, Veterinary Officers, Environmental Protection Officers, etc. The Ghana Police Service also performs key roles in the country's efforts to manage international migration. Even though they are not part of the frontline border control personnel, they are often responsible for the arrest and prosecution of immigrants involved in irregular migration or criminal activities.

Chapter 2. Right to Enter the Country

82. Article 21(1)(g) of the *1992 Constitution* of Ghana provides that 'all persons shall have the right to freedom of movement which means the right to move freely in Ghana, the right to leave and enter Ghana and immunity from expulsion from Ghana'. This right is not absolute. Article 21(4)(d) claws back and derogates from the above right by permitting 'the imposition of restriction[s] on the freedom of entry into Ghana, or movement in Ghana, of a person who is not a citizen of Ghana'. But any such restriction must be done under the authority of a law, and must be reasonably justifiable in terms of the spirit of the *Constitution*.

§1. Conditions for the Right to Enter

I. Prohibition of Entry

83. Immigrants may be allowed entry into Ghana if they do not fall within the category of prohibited immigrants as defined by section 8(1) of the *Immigration Act, 2000 (Act 573)* and they satisfy immigration requirements at the point of entry, provided, that the possession of the appropriate documents does not confer a right of entry. A *prohibited immigrant* is a person other than a citizen of Ghana who (i) has a deportation order in force against him made under *Act 573* or any other enactment; (ii) is unable to show that he has the means of sup porting himself and his dependants if any, or is destitute and likely to be a burden on public funds; (iii) refuses to submit to a medical examination after being required to do so by a health officer; (iv) has been sentenced in a foreign country for any extraditable crime within the meaning of the Extradition Act of Ghana; (v) has been certified by a health officer to be medically unfit to enter Ghana; (vi) has been declared by the Minister by executive instrument to be a person whose entry into Ghana is not conducive to the public good; (vii) procures or attempts to bring into Ghana any person for the purpose of prostitution or other immoral purpose; (viii) is a person whose activities are contrary to the laws of Ghana; or (ix) is the dependent of a person to whom any of the preceding provisions applies.

II. Pre-entry Conditions

A. Possession of Travel Document and Entry Visa

84. Section 4 of *Act 573* requires that, unless exempted, all persons entering Ghana must possess a valid passport or Travel Document and a valid entry visa or emergency entry permit issued by the competent national or international authorities recognized by the Government of Ghana.

B. Exemptions

85. Persons who enjoy an exempt status do not require entry visas by reason of treaty or other obligation assumed by Ghana. An exempted person includes nationals of the fifteen Member States of the ECOWAS under the relevant ECOWAS Protocols, Malaysia and Kenya. The fifteen Member States of ECOWAS are Benin, Burkina Faso, Cape Verde, Cote d'Ivoire, Gambia, Ghana, Guinea, Guinea Bissau, Liberia, Mali, Niger, Nigeria, Senegal, Sierra Leone, and Togo. Although *Act 573* does not specifically provide for ECOWAS citizens, *Regulations 3 and 8* of the *Immigration Regulations, 2001 (L.I. 1691)* make provision for ECOWAS citizens in fulfilment of Ghana's international obligations under the ECOWAS Treaty and Protocols on migration. Under the 1972 ECOWAS Treaty, the Revised ECOWAS Treaty of 1997, the *Protocol on the Free Movement of Persons, Right of Residence and Establishment of 1979* and the several Protocols relating thereto, ECOWAS nationals are admitted into Ghana without any visa requirements whatsoever. The 1979 *Protocol on the Free Movement of Persons, Right of Residence and Establishment* provides a maximum of ninety days visitor's permit, and it is subject to renewal when an applicant provides reasonable grounds to justify the request for renewal.

86. Regulation 21 of *L.I. 1691* provides details of persons who are exempted from entry visas to include (1) a citizen of Ghana or (2) a foreigner who is not a prohibited immigrant and is (i) a citizen of a country with which Ghana has concluded a reciprocal visa exemption agreement; (ii) a member of the diplomatic or consular service of a foreign country who is duly accredited to the Republic by the government of the country concerned; (iii) an official of an international organization who is entitled to diplomatic privileges by or under the provisions of any enactment; (iv) a person granted diplomatic status by the Republic; (v) a person in the employment of the Republic; (vi) the wife of a specified category of persons (vii) a member of the armed forces of a friendly power entering Ghana on duty by permission of the Ghana Government; or (viii) a person in respect of whom the Minister has granted a waiver. Any of the above categories of persons shall be permitted to enter and remain in Ghana. Where such a visa exempted person who has been permitted to enter the country ceases while in the country to possess the qualifications by virtue of which he was given the exemption, that person shall be required to appear before an immigration officer as though that person were entering the country for the first time.

C. Visa

1. Entry Visas

87. Section 4 of *Act 573* provides that all foreigners entering Ghana require entry visas unless specifically exempted from obtaining a visa to enter Ghana. An entry visa may be obtained abroad prior to arrival in Ghana from a Ghana Embassy, High Commission or Consulate. Where Ghana has no Consular or Diplomatic rep resentation, an application for entry visa may be made to the nearest British Diplomatic Mission or Consulate authorized by the Government of Ghana to act on its behalf.

88. Where a person who appears before an immigration officer does not have a visa or an emergency entry permit, the immigration officer may grant that person an entry visa subject to the conditions prescribed by the Regulations, and to any other conditions that the immigration officer may impose. However, an application for emergency visa should have been filed with the Director of Immigration on the foreign national's behalf by the host of that foreigner. According to Regulation 4 of *L.I. 1691*, such an emergency entry visa is valid for fourteen days, and may be granted if the immigration officer is satisfied that the foreign national is (a) not a prohibited immigrant; (b) in possession of a valid passport or travel document; (c) is proceeding from a country where Ghana has no diplomatic mission or consulate; or (d) where Ghana has a representative, but the entry into Ghana is being sought for an emergency assignment.

89. An application for an emergency visa filed with the Director of Immigration on the foreign national's behalf by his or her host should indicate the foreign national's personal details including: nationality, place of residence in Ghana, occupation or business to be followed or undertaken while in Ghana; particulars of passport; proposed date of arrival; purpose of visit and duration of stay; an undertaking by the applicant to return, as well as a statement that the applicant will not undertake or participate in any activity which might offend the religious beliefs of any section of the community. In the case of a passenger passing through Ghana, the route to be followed must also be indicated. Such a foreign national should provide a security furnished by bond, deposit or a letter of guarantee by the person who guarantees his or her visit. Any pass granted to the applicant shall be a Form C pass, as set out in the Schedule.

2. Ghana Visa

90. A Ghana entry visa is an authority or permit issued to foreigners who wish or desire to enter into, or transit through Ghana's territory. The basic objectives of Ghana's entry visa policy are to facilitate the entry of genuine travellers while managing the associated risks; and to contribute to building strong international links, promoting tourism, investment, and addressing skills shortages. There are two main categories of Ghana entry visas, namely diplomatic and ordinary visas, and they are granted based on the applicant's identity, purpose of visit and type of passport.

3. Diplomatic Visa

91. Diplomatic visa are issued to members of the diplomatic or consular services of a foreign country who are duly accredited to Ghana by the government of the country concerned i.e., Ambassadors, High Commissioners, Public Ministers,

Career Diplomats or Consular Officers, etc., as well as officials of international organizations who are entitled to diplomatic privileges by, or under the provisions of any enactment, such as the United Nations and its specialized Agencies, World Bank officials on official duty or assignment in Ghana, etc. The members of immediate families of these categories are also granted diplomatic visas: These are coded as A1, A2 and A3, and are issued free of charge.

4. Ordinary Visa

92. Ordinary visas are issued to several sub-categories of visa which can be issued to foreigners who visit Ghana for business reasons, tourism or holidays, temporary employment, or who travel through Ghana on transit. These visas are coded in accordance with the type or nature of the visit. The most common types of ordinary visa are: B-1 (Business visa); B-2 (Holiday/Tourist Visa); C-1/C-2 (Transit Visa); D (Crew Visa); F-1/F-2 (Student Visa); H-1–H-4 (Temporary Workers Visa).

Summary

93. Subject to the conditions of *Act 573* and *L.I. 1691*, any person seeking to enter into Ghana must possess a valid passport or other travel document and a valid visa, or must have been exempted from obtaining a visa to enter Ghana. Alternatively, he must have his name endorsed upon a visa and is in the company of the holder of the visa or must have applied and been granted an emergency entry permit or must have been admitted because of his diplomatic status by the Government of Ghana. Thus, all foreigners seeking permission to enter Ghana require Ghana entry visa unless otherwise exempted. Such exempted persons include nationals of the fifteen Member States of the ECOWAS, Malaysia and Kenya. A person in possession of travel documents issued by the Government of Ghana does not need a visa to enter Ghana. Ghanaian citizens do not require visa to enter the country.

§2. Administrative Procedures and Documents

I. General Provisions

94. The GIS is the frontline agency responsible for the entry, residence and employment of foreign nationals in Ghana in accordance with the provisions of the *Immigration Act, 2000(Act 573)* and the *Immigration Regulations, 2001 (L.I. 1691)*. The Immigration Regulations provide detailed rules, procedures, forms and documents to aid the implementation of the provisions of *Act 573*. The GIS Act, and the notices, instructions, and other orders from the Service also provide administrative guidance.

Regulation 4(1)(d) of *L.I. 1691* provides the entry visa requirements. A visa may be obtained from Ghana Embassies/High Commissions, Consulates or other Embas sies authorized by the Government of Ghana to issue visas on her behalf. An application for an entry visa into Ghana shall be made to the Director of Immigration or the representative of the Director.

95. An emergency entry permit valid for fourteen days may be obtained at the point of entry if an application has been filed out on behalf of the foreign national by foreign national's host with the Director of Immigration indicating:

- personal details including nationality and the place of residence in Ghana;
- the occupation or business to be followed or undertaken while Ghana;
- particulars of the passport;
- the proposed date of arrival;
- the purpose of visit and the duration of stay;
- a statement to the effect that the applicant will not undertake or participate in any activities which might offend the religious beliefs or any section of the community;
- if passing through Ghana, the route to be followed; and
- a commitment made by the applicant to return any pass granted;
- the furnishing of security by bond, deposit or a letter of guarantee from the person who guarantees the foreign national visit.

If an applicant for an emergency entry visa is a national of a country where Ghana has a representation, but the emergency entry visa for Ghana is being sought for an emergency assignment, then he must satisfy the additional condition that the distance between the place of abode and the Ghana Consular office should be such that the impromptu nature of the journey did not allow the person to travel to the office for a visa, that the applicant is proceeding to Ghana at such short notice for business transactions, that the applicant is a guest of the government or a member of a delegation which is coming to Ghana at the instance of the government at short notice, or that the entry permit of an applicant who is a person resident in Ghana has expired while the applicant was outside Ghana.

The Entry Process

96. In sections 1–4 of *Act 573*, a person in charge of a sea-going vessel, aircraft or vehicle arriving at any port or place in Ghana shall not permit a passenger who embarked outside Ghana to disembark until disembarkation has been authorized by the immigration officer. A person entering Ghana has to enter at an authorized point and proceed to the nearest immigration office, produce his travel document and complete the prescribed forms. If the person arrives by sea or air in Ghana at a place other than an authorized place or port, such a person should, within forty-eight hours, proceed and report to the immigration officer at the nearest immigration post. An immigration officer to whom a person reports shall, if the person is not prohibited from entering Ghana and he is satisfied by documentary or other evidence of the person's identity, grant that person entry subject to the provisions of *Act 573*. An immigration officer may dispense with the personal attendance of any person if he is satisfied by documentary or other evidence of that person's identity and right to enter Ghana. Any person who does not comply with this section commits an offence and is liable on summary conviction to a fine or imprisonment for a term not exceeding twelve months or to both.

97. A person shall not enter Ghana except by one of the approved places of entry into Ghana, which includes (a) a place in Ghana in respect of which landing or docking rights have been granted to an aircraft or vessel; or (b) a place specified in the Schedule to *Act 573*. Without prejudice to any other penalty imposed by or under *Act 573*, a person who uses an unapproved place to enter Ghana commits an offence and is liable on summary conviction to a fine or to a term of imprisonment of not less than three months and not exceeding twelve months or to both.

98. An immigration officer may permit a person, other than a citizen of Ghana, to enter Ghana for a period that may be specified, only where the officer is satisfied that the person entering Ghana is in possession of a valid passport or other travel document and a valid visa to enter Ghana where applicable; or is exempted from obtaining a visa to enter Ghana; or has his name endorsed upon a visa and is in the company of the holder of the visa; or has applied and been granted an emergency entry permit; or is a person admitted to diplomatic status by the Government of Ghana. Where a person who appears before an immigration officer does not have a visa or an emergency entry permit, the immigration officer may nevertheless grant him a visa subject to prescribed conditions.

99. Where an immigration officer is in doubt as to the right of any person to enter Ghana, the officer may detain that person who will remain in custody pending the determination of the matter. The Director may, pending the completion of enquiries in respect of a detained person, release that person from custody upon such directions as he may determine and may for that purpose, issue a temporary permit to that person. A person who refuses or neglects to comply with a direction given by an immigration officer in such cases or who leaves the detention area in contravention of sub-section (1) commits an offence and is liable on summary conviction to a fine or imprisonment for a term not exceeding twelve months or both.

II. Visitors

100. According to Regulation 8 of *L.I. 1691*, having obtained the requisite visa, a visitor must satisfy the immigration officer on arrival that he is genuinely seeking entry for a limited period as stated by him, and that he will leave Ghana at the end of the period granted him. Other conditions include the assurance that on entry, he will not take up any employment while residing in Ghana on a visitor's permit, he does not intend to study at any educational institution, and he will not become a burden on public funds. Regulation 8(2) of *L.I. 1691* provides that 'A visitor's visa shall be subject to the condition that the person to whom it is granted shall not undertake or follow any occupation for reward, except such as may be specified in the visa'. After entry is allowed at the point of entry, a maximum of sixty days stay (ninety days in the case of ECOWAS nationals) is granted. Extension of the duration of the stay is allowed provided that the approving officer is convinced that the conditions for extension have been met.

III. Visitors in Transit

101. A person seeking entry clearance to enter Ghana in transit and is not a prohibited immigrant may be admitted for a period not exceeding forty-eight hours. The immigration officer at the point of entry must be satisfied that:

- the visitor has a valid visa and is assured of entry into the destination country;
- the visitor is exempted from sustaining himself in the transit and destination countries;
- the visitor will not decide to terminate his journey in the transit country, and that;
- passengers in transit without an entry visa are permitted to enter Ghana for the purpose of visiting places of interest.

102. The Director or any immigration officer authorized by him may, before issuing a permit or visa under L.I. 1691, make enquiries or require the production of evidence in order to be satisfied as to the truth of any statement made in the application for the permit. Any person who violates these provisions commits an offence and is liable, on summary conviction, to pay a fine or a period imprisonment not exceeding twelve months or to both.

103. The above-mentioned processes and procedures do not apply to any person who enters Ghana in direct transit to a place outside Ghana when that person arrives by (a) vessel which is proceeding to a place outside Ghana and does not disembark from the vessel; (b) aircraft, and does not leave the transit area of the airport and leaves Ghana within twenty-four hours after arrival on the same aircraft or another aircraft; or (c) vehicle, vessel or aircraft and is escorted by an immigration officer from the point of entry to the exit point and leaves Ghana within forty-eight hours after arrival.

IV. Crew Members

104. Section 42 of the *Immigration Act, 2000 (Act 573)* provides various exemptions, in terms of passport and visa requirements, to the entry conditions for certain special classes of people like crew members of vessels. Under section 42 of the *Immigration Act*, members of the crew of a vessel or aircraft arriving in Ghana from abroad may be permitted to enter Ghana upon presentation of satisfactory proof of their identity notwithstanding the fact that they may not have a passport, visa, or permit. No member of the crew of a vessel or aircraft shall be discharged or left behind in Ghana without the consent of an immigration officer. These rules in section 42 of the *Immigration Act* do not apply to a member of the crew of a vessel or aircraft who is a citizen of Ghana.

V. Immigration Regulations

105. Detailed procedural and administrative requirements for entry into Ghana can also be found in various sections of the *Immigration Regulations, 2001 (L.I. 1691)*. Under *Regulation 1* entitled '*Examination and Condition of Entry*', an immigration officer may interview persons entering Ghana or applying for permission or renewal of permission to enter Ghana. Form A in the Schedule (Disembarkation) is used for the entry examination. *Regulation 2* requires a person entering or leaving Ghana; or applying for permission or renewal of permission to be or remain in Ghana to produce their passport to the immigration officer for inspection and stamping where necessary. A foreign national must any time when so requested by an immigration officer of the rank of Inspector or above, produce his passport for inspection.

106. Regulation 3 is entitled '*Visa and Entry Permits*'. It provides that a foreign national, except one from an ECOWAS country, entering Ghana shall have stamped or affixed in that person's passport a visa valid from the date on which the foreign national enters Ghana. A foreign national who is an exempted person is not required to have a visa for entry into Ghana. This is also the case for a foreign national who is in the possession of travel documents issued by the Government of Ghana. An application for an entry visa for Ghana is made to the Director or the representative of the Director using Form B in the Schedule.

107. Emergency Entry Visas are provided for under *Regulation 4*. The conditions for the grant of emergency entry visas are discussed in paragraphs 87 under *Entry Visas* and 94 under *General Provisions supra.*

108. The information required on the application for an emergency entry visa is also provided for in *Regulation 4*. These details are discussed in paragraph 87 under *Entry Visas supra.*

109. Regulation 5 deals with *Re-entry Visa*. A foreign national who is lawfully in Ghana and who seeks to leave Ghana temporarily, must, apply to the Director of Immigration for a re-entry visa indicating in the application the reason for wishing to re-enter Ghana; the proposed length of stay in Ghana; whether or not the foreign national is in possession of a valid return and onward ticket, and evidence of sufficient funds.

110. Transit Visa and Permit processes are provided for in *Regulations 6 and 7 of* The *Immigration Regulations, 2001 (L.I. 1691)*.An immigration officer may issue a transit visa to a person who intends to pass through Ghana in transit. A transit visa is issued for a period determined by the immigration officer, but never exceeds a period of forty-eight hours. A transit visa can be issued subject to the condition that the person does not undertake or pursue any occupation for reward. Where a passenger who arrives in Ghana in transit without an entry visa applies for leave to enter the country for the purpose of seeing places of interest, an immigration officer may, subject to the payment of the prescribed fee, grant the passenger a transit per mit to enter the country provided that the passenger is in possession of a return or onward ticket and provides evidence of adequate funds for the purpose of the transit visit. A transit permit granted to any person is valid for a maximum period of forty-eight hours and can only be issued at air, land and sea ports.

111. Regulation 8 of L.I. 1691 deals with *Visitor's Visa*. In any situation where a transit visa, a residence permit, an indefinite residence or a right of abode status respectively is inapplicable, the immigration officer can grant a visitor's visa. A visitor's visa is issued subject to certain conditions provided for under the heading *Visitor's Visa* (*see* paragraph 100 *supra*).

112. If a person seeking entry permission is required to furnish security in respect of that person's repatriation expenses, the immigration officer may, pursuant to *Regulation 14*, require a bond for the sum determined; a deposit of the sum determined with the immigration officer; or a letter of guarantee for the sum determined. The sum determined shall be a sum equivalent to the cost of sending the foreign national and dependants of the national from a suitable place in Ghana to the country of origin; or at the discretion of the Director to some other country where that national and the dependants of that person will be admitted in addition to any further sum that may be required for any other related purpose. Where a person furnishes security by deposit, the immigration officer shall give that person a receipt for the sum deposited, and when the person leaves Ghana permanently, or is repatriated the immigration officer shall return the sum deposited or the balance remaining after deduction of the deportation expenses to the person who made the deposit.

Chapter 3. Refusal of Entry

113. Travellers are not allowed to enter Ghana if they fall within the category of prohibited immigrants and/or if they do not satisfy immigration requirements at the point of entry. The Immigration Service cannot be held financially liable for the repatriation of such persons. The carrier, master or agents of the aircraft, vessel, or vehicle are individually or collectively responsible for the immediate removal of such a traveller from Ghana and carrier liability will be established where applicable. Section 8 of *Act 573* defines a prohibited immigrant as a person other than a citizen of Ghana who (i) has a deportation order in force against him made under *Act 573* or any other enactment; (ii) is unable to show that he has the means of supporting himself and his dependants if any, or is destitute and likely to be a burden on the public; (iii) refuses to submit to a medical examination after being required to do so by a health officer; (iv) has been sentenced in a foreign country for any extraditable crime within the Extradition Act of Ghana; (v) has been certified by a health officer to be medically unfit to enter Ghana; (vi) has been declared by the Minister by executive instrument to be a person whose entry into Ghana is not conducive to the public good; (vii) procures or attempts to bring into Ghana any person for the purpose of prostitution or other immoral purpose; (viii) a person whose activities are contrary to the laws of Ghana; or (ix) the dependent of a person to whom any of the preceding provisions applies.

114. A person who enters Ghana while he is a prohibited immigrant commits an offence and is liable on summary conviction to a fine or to imprisonment for a term of not less than six months and not exceeding two years or to both. Where a person is charged with an offence as a prohibited immigrant, the burden of proof that he is not a prohibited immigrant lies upon that person.

115. According to section 8(4) of *Act 573*, an immigration officer may prevent a prohibited immigrant from entering Ghana, or, if he has already entered Ghana, direct him to depart from Ghana by the first available means, and may use all force necessary to ensure compliance with his orders; order a prohibited immigrant not to disembark from any ship, vehicle or aircraft on which he may be, or not to depart from any place where he may be, unless travelling to some other place approved by the immigration officer. The person to whom the order has been issued is deemed to be in lawful custody. An immigration officer can arrest a prohibited immigrant without warrant and effectuate his repatriation or arraign him before a court for an offence. Where an immigration officer directs a prohibited immigrant to leave Ghana by the first available means, he may, at the same time, order the person in charge or the owner or agent of any vessel, vehicle or aircraft from which the prohibited immigrant disembarked to remove him from Ghana by the first available means. A person who fails to comply with an order given by an immigration officer to remove a prohibited immigrant from the territory of Ghana commits an offence and is liable, on summary conviction, to a fine or a term imprisonment not exceeding twelve months or both.

Part II. Right of Residence: General Provisions

Chapter 1. Short Stay

§1. Conditions for Short Stay

I. General Provisions

116. Permits granted on arrival to foreigners to enter and remain in Ghana for a short period are categorized as *transit and visitor's permits*. The *Immigration Act, 2000(Act 573)* provides the requirements for appearance before an immigration officer on arrival, who may upon being satisfied by documentary or other evidence as presented to him or her of the person's identity, grant that person entry permission as stipulated in section 2 of that Act. According to section 4 of *Act 573*, a potential entrant must possess a valid passport or other travel document and a valid visa. A Ghana entry visa is an authority or permit issued to foreigners who wish or desire to enter into, or transit through Ghana's territory. Depending on the applicant's identity, purpose of visit and type of passport, the Ghana entry visa may be either a diplomatic visa or an ordinary visa. The ordinary visa is classified as: B-1 (Business visa), B-2 (Holiday/Tourist Visa), C-1 and C-2 (Transit Visa), D (Crew Visa), F-1 F-2 (Student Visa), H-1–H-4 (Temporary Workers Visa).

117. The visa should be endorsed on a valid passport or travel document issued by a competent national or international authority recognized by the Government of Ghana. Conditions for the issuance of an emergency entry visa are discussed in paragraphs 87 under *Entry Visas* and 94 under *General Provisions supra*.

II. Transit Permit

118. A person, seeking entry clearance to enter Ghana in transit and is not a prohibited immigrant *may be admitted for a period not exceeding forty-eight hours* subject to conditions provided for in *Regulation 6 of L.I. 1691* as follows:

1. An immigration officer may issue a transit visa to a person who intends to pass through Ghana in transit.
2. A transit visa shall be for a period determined by the immigration officer but shall not exceed forty-eight hours.

Further conditions for the grant of a transit visa are discussed in paragraphs 101 and 110 *supra*. An application for an extension of stay beyond forty-eight hours may be refused unless circumstances beyond the control of the visitor have arisen e.g., where there is no flight available.

119. Passengers who arrive in Ghana in transit without an entry visa or permit may be allowed to enter for a short stay for the purpose of visiting places of interest and tourist sites. This is governed by *Regulation 7 of L.I. 1691* which provides that:

1. Where a passenger who arrives in Ghana in transit without an entry visa applies for leave to enter the country for the purpose of seeing places of interest, an immigration officer may, subject to the payment of the prescribed fee, grant the passenger a transit permit to enter the country provided that the passenger
   a. is in possession of a return or onward ticket; and
   b. provides evidence of adequate funds, for the purpose of the transit visit.
2. A transit permit, granted to any person under sub-regulation (1) shall be for a maximum period of forty-eight hours.
3. A transit permit is granted only at air, land and sea ports.

The transit permit fee applicable to a person other than an ECOWAS national in 2016 was USD 20.

III. Visitors Permit

120. All foreign travellers who satisfy the relevant entry requirements can be granted a visitor's permit to enter and remain in Ghana for a temporary period not exceeding two months or sixty days, and, in the case of ECOWAS, nationals not exceeding three months or ninety days, as provided for in the ECOWAS Treaty. A visitor's visa is issued subject to the condition that the visitor grantee shall not undertake or pursue an occupation for reward, unless specified in the visa as provided in *Regulation 8 of L.I. 1691*. A visitor's permit can be extended on application to the Director of Immigration or the nearest Regional Immigration Office. An extension of stay as a visitor is refused if it is established that any of the requirements above was breached or not satisfied.

121. In accordance with *Regulation 8 of L.I. 1691*, the immigration officer may grant a visitor's visa subject to the condition that such a visitor shall not follow or pursue an occupation for reward while visiting Ghana on a visitor's permit, unless specified otherwise in the visa. Having obtained the requisite visa, a visitor must satisfy the immigration officer on arrival that he is genuinely seeking entry for a limited period as stated by him; and that he will leave Ghana at the end of the period granted him. A visitor must also satisfy the immigration officer that he does not intend to study at an institution for education and will not become a burden on the public funds. Permission for a maximum of sixty days stay (ninety days in the case of ECOWAS nationals) is granted at the point of entry. Extension of the duration of stay can be granted if the approving officer is convinced that the conditions set out above are met.

§2. Administrative Procedures and Documents

122. The administrative procedure governing the issuing of visa for a short stay in Ghana is provided for in Regulation 4(1)(d) of the *Immigration Regulations, 2001 (L.I. 1691)*. A visa may be obtained from Ghana Embassies/High Commissions, Consulates or other Embassies authorized by the Government of Ghana to issue visas on her behalf. Emergency Entry Permits valid for fourteen days can be obtained where an application has been filed on behalf of the foreign national by the host with the Director of Immigration, as discussed under *Short Stay supra*. If a passenger is passing through Ghana, the route to be followed and undertaken commitment made by the applicant to return any pass that is granted to him is required. In such cases security can be required, furnished by bond, deposit, or a letter of guarantee by the person who guarantees the foreign national's visit. A transit permit can be issued after the fee as provided for in Regulation 7(1) of *L.I.1691* has been paid.

123. Extensions to the initial sixty or ninety day visitor's permit may be granted on application. The GIS can extend visitor permits by a minimum of three months and a maximum of six months. When applying for extension or stay, visitors are to:

- complete the requisite application forms which can be obtained from the Immigration Headquarters or the nearest Regional Command of the Service;
- provide two current passport-sized photographs;
- write an application letter stating reason(s) for the request (i.e., visitors who wish to stay for a period more than three months);
- provide a valid return ticket or any form of guarantee that the visitor will leave the country at the end of the period requested for;
- provide documentary evidence of intent to invest in Ghana (applicable to would-be investors only);
- provide a valid passport; and
- pay the requisite processing fee and the prescribed fees for a residence permit.

An application for the extension of a short stay visa attracts graded monthly fees for dependents, Ghanaians with foreign passports, ECOWAS nationals and other non-nationals.

124. According to Regulation 5 of *L.I. 1691*, a foreign national who is lawfully in Ghana and who seeks to leave Ghana temporarily, must, for the purposes of section 5(1) of the Act, apply to the Director of Immigration for a re-entry visa indicating the following issues in the application:

(a) the reason for wishing to re-enter Ghana;

(b) the proposed length of stay in Ghana;
(c) whether or not the foreign national is in possession of a valid return and onward ticket, and
(d) evidence of sufficient funds.

The application for a re-entry visa is to be made using Form D in the Schedule of *L.I. 1691*.

§3. Legal Position

125. A person who has been granted a permit to remain in Ghana may, within one month before the permit expires, apply to the Director in the prescribed manner for a renewal of the permit (section 23 of *Act 573*).Any person other than a prohibited immigrant affected by a refusal to grant or renew a permit under this Act or revocation of a permit under this Act by an immigration officer may submit a petition to the Minister within seven days of such action. Subject to the prescribed procedure the Minister, takes such action as he considers appropriate (*section 46 of Act 573*).According to section 47 *of Act 573*, a petition to the Minister under section 46 does not stay the execution of the action which has been petitioned against. However there are regulations that provide conditions that enable a person to be granted permission to stay in Ghana pending the hearing of a petition made by that person.

126. According to section 49 of *Act 573*, some areas in Ghana may be designated as prohibited to foreign nationals. The relevant section provides that: (1) The Minister may by legislative instrument declare some areas in Ghana as prohibited to foreign nationals. (2) A foreign national shall not enter or remain in areas prohibited to foreigners unless he has a valid prohibited area permit granted by the appropriate authority. (3) A permit granted under sub-section (2) shall be subject to such conditions as may be specified in the permit and prescribed by the Regulations, and shall be issued in the prescribed form. (4) A person who contravenes sub-section (2) commits an offence and is on summary conviction, liable to a term of imprisonment of not less than three months or to a fine or to both.

§4. Position of Family Members

127. First degree family members of those granted diplomatic visa are also granted a diplomatic visa. These are coded A1, A2, A3, and are issued free of charge. There are no special provisions for the family members of those who enter Ghana for a short period and, therefore, it can be inferred that, family members of such people must go through the normal process, as explained *supra*, to be granted permission to enter the country. If a permit is revoked, the revocation applies to: *(a) the person whose name is endorsed in the permit, (b) the spouse of the holder of the permit where the spouse was issued the permit as a consequence of the issuing of a permit to the other spouse, and (c) a dependant of the holder of the permit who is not a citizen* (section 20(5) of *Act 573*). Notification of the revocation to the holder of the permit constitutes a notification to the person's family members (spouse and non-citizen dependants of that person), as mentioned *supra* (section 20(6) of *Act 573*).

Chapter 2. Residence

128. In accordance with section 13 of *Act 573*, a person who has been lawfully entered Ghana can, upon an application to the Director in the prescribed manner, be issued a residence permit. This is confirmed by Regulation 9 of *L.I.1691* which provides that the Director of Immigration may grant a residence permit to a foreign national who intends to remain in Ghana for a substantial period.

§1. Conditions for Residence

129. According to section 13(2) of *Act 573*, the Director may grant a residence permit for up to a period not exceeding eight years, subject to the condition that a residence permit is not issued for more than four years in first instance. *Regulation 9 of the Immigration Regulation 2001, L.I.1691*, also sets out that a residence permit is granted subject to the condition that the person to whom it is granted shall not undertake any employment or engage in any business, trade or profession unless specified in the permit. A person may therefore lawfully embark on any business or profession specified in a permit. This can either be for business or study purposes. A residence permit is initially issued for a period not exceeding four years and can be extended for another four year period. Regulation 9 of *L.I.1691* makes provision for the extension of the initial four year validity period of a residence permit if the Director is satisfied that the person has fulfilled all the conditions of the previous permit and has not abused any privilege granted to him or her under the previous permit.

§2. Administrative Procedures and Documents

130. Regulation 9 of *L.I. 1691* and Form E of its Schedule detail the procedure and documentary requirements that must be complied with when applying for a residence permit in Ghana. The requirements are:

- recent passport photographs;
- a photocopy of approval of the Immigrant Quota, Company Tax Clearance Certificate from IRS;
- a bond to be executed (where applicable);
- copies of the marriage/birth certificate (where applicable);
- a sworn affidavit (where applicable);
- a letter of support from the GIPC, GFZB, (where applicable);
- a police clearance report from home country;
- a medical Report; and
- Company Registration Documents, a Work contract document or appointment letter (where applicable).

131. According to section 20(1) of *Act 573*, a person may not remain in Ghana after the expiration of a permit issued to that person. All foreign nationals legally resident in Ghana are required to notify the Director of the Immigration Service of the expiry of their residence permit if they are remaining outside of Ghana for an indefinite period. Failure to comply with this obligation is subject to the payment of penalties. The penalty for an expired residence permit (per month) is GHS 10.00 for dependants of Ghanaians with foreign passports. Short stay visitors may apply for renewal of the stay or petition the Minister upon refusal to renew or grant them a permit (sections 23 and 46 of *Act 573*).

§3. Legal Position of Residents

132. According to section 23 of *Act 573*, a person who has been granted a permit to remain in Ghana may, within one month before the permit expires, apply to the Director in the prescribed manner for a renewal of the permit the permit. Under section 46 of *Act 573*, any person other than a prohibited immigrant affected by a refusal to grant or renew a permit or the revocation of a permit by an immigration officer can submit a petition to the Minister within seven days of such action. Subject to the prescribed procedure, the Minister takes such action as he considers appropriate. According to section 49 of *Act 573*, some areas in Ghana may be designated as prohibited to foreign nationals. The relevant section provides as follows:

(1) The Minister may by legislative instrument declare some areas in Ghana as prohibited to foreign nationals.
(2) A foreign national shall not enter or remain in areas prohibited to foreigners unless he has a valid prohibited area permit granted by the appropriate authority.
(3) A permit granted under sub-section (2) shall be subject to such conditions as may be specified in the permit and prescribed by Regulations made under section 55 of this Act in a prescribed form.
(4) A person who contravenes sub-section (2) commits an offence and is, on summary conviction, liable to a term of imprisonment of no less than three months, a fine or to both.

133. The *1992 Constitution* and Immigration laws of Ghana give residents access to the rights that Ghanaians enjoy, albeit with some limitations and strict procedural processes in some cases, e.g., the right to own real estate and to employment. With regard to real estate, Article 266(4) of Ghana's Constitution limits the right or interest that can be enjoyed in land or real estate in Ghana for a non-citizen or resident foreigner, to leasehold for a term of no more than fifty years at a time. Such leases can be renewed repeatedly time and again without any restriction. Nevertheless, Article 266(1) of Ghana's *1992 Constitution* prohibits the granting a freehold interest in any land or real estate in Ghana to non-citizens or foreigners. So even though a resident can acquire real estate in Ghana on leasehold with a constitutionally specified maximum duration of fifty years at a time, he or she cannot be vested with freehold interest in or rights over any land in Ghana.

134. Residents have the right to send their children to school, to pursue education at all levels, but they do have to pay the fees as prescribed for foreign students. They have the right of access to the health service as well as other utility and municipal services at the requisite fees or costs.

135. On the right to employment, section 27(3) of the *Immigration Act 2000, (Act 573)* provides that the Minister may issue a work permit to any person who is not a prohibited immigrant, a visitor, tourist, transit passenger or student, and who satisfies the Immigrant Quota Committee that (a) he wishes to enter Ghana in order to take up work or employment; (b) he is qualified to work or undertake employment in the trade, business or calling in respect of which the application is made; (c) his taking up of the work or employment will be to the benefit generally of Ghana; and (d) he is lawfully resident in Ghana and is qualified to work as an employee or a self-employed person. Along these lines, section 24 of *Act 573* stipulates that a person shall not employ any foreign national in Ghana except in accordance with a permit granted by the Immigrant Quota Committee. Further, section 28 of the *GIPC Act, 2013 (Act 865)* stipulates that foreign nationals shall not be eligible to participate in a business enterprise in Ghana except where they have made specified minimum capital investments in relation to those business enterprises, which must not be enterprises reserved for Ghanaians.

136. A resident who seeks to work as a self-employed person must take into consideration the *Ghana Investment Promotion Act, 2013 (Act 865),* in particular, its section 27 which reserves certain business activities exclusively for Ghanaians (*see* paragraph 40 *supra*). Section 28 of *Act 865* gives minimum foreign capital investment requirements for an enterprise in which foreign participation is permitted (*see* paragraph 41 *supra*).

§4. Position of Family Members of Residents

137. A foreigner who is resident in Ghana can be accompanied by his or her dependents, who are not permitted to undertake or pursue any occupation for reward. The interpretation section of the *Immigration Act, 2000, (Act 573)*, defines dependents to include the spouse and child or children. A child is a person below the age of 18 years. The number of years the spouse and children may spend in Ghana depends on the remaining years the spouse or parent can spend in Ghana subject, however, to renewal. Detailed requirements and conditions are provided for in Regulation 9 of *L.I. 1691*, as follows: 'the Director may issue a residence permit to the spouse, or other dependants of a person to whom a residence permit has been issued (referred to as the principal holder) subject to the condition that the person to whom it is issued shall not undertake or follow any occupation for reward. A residence permit granted to a principal holder's dependant shall be for a period not exceeding that applicable to the principal holder's permit or the residue of the principal holder's permit.'

Requirements: Spouse

- A letter applying for residence permit from spouse.
- A filled in residence permit application form.
- A photocopy of the marriage certificate, which must be translated into English if in another language.
- Two passport size photographs.
- A bond to be executed by the spouse and a second guarantor.
- Photocopies of the bio data pages of both guarantors' passports (Ghanaian).
- Proof of the spouse's means of livelihood, financial support.
- The prescribed fees must have been paid.

Children under Eighteen (18) Years

- A letter of application from a biological parent/guardian.
- A guarantor (Ghanaian) who in addition to parent or guardian must sign a bond in the presence of an Immigration Officer.
- A photocopy of the bio data pages of the parent/guardian and second guarantor's Ghanaian passports.
- The guardian must submit a sworn affidavit with a seal from the high Court.
- A photocopy of the child's birth certificate.
- A letter of consent from biological parent.
- A filled in Residence Permit (RP) application form.
- Two passport size photographs.
- A letter from school, if applicable.
- The prescribed fees must have been paid.

138. In cases where a permit of the principal holder is revoked, the revocation may also apply to the spouse and children or dependents of the principal holder. Such revocation applies to: *(a) the person whose name is endorsed in the permit of the principal holder, (b) the spouse of the holder of the permit where the spouse was issued the permit as consequence of the issuing of a permit to the other spouse, and (c) the dependant of the holder of the permit who is not a citizen* (section 20(5) of *Act 573*). Notification of a revocation to the holder of the permit also constitutes notification to the person's family members (as endorsed therein, i.e., the spouse and non-citizen dependants), as mentioned *supra* (section 20(6) of *Act 573*).

Chapter 3. Long-Term Residence

§1. Conditions for Long-Term Residence

139. *Act 573* has two main categories of long-term residence status. These are *indefinite residence status* and *right of abode* which may be conferred on foreign nationals. A person who has resided in Ghana for a specified number of years, is of a good character and intends to reside permanently in Ghana as stipulated in section 15 of *Act 573* may apply for an indefinite residence status. A Ghanaian who by any reason has lost his Ghanaian citizenship and people of African descent in the Diaspora may apply for a right of abode status. The interpretation section of *Act 573*, section 56, defines a person of African descent in the Diaspora as a person whose immediate ancestors have not resided on the African continent for at least three generations, but whose origin, either by documentary proof or by ethnic characteristics, is African. Sections 14 and 17 of *Act 573* provide for indefinite residence status and right of abode status respectively.

I. Indefinite Residence Status

140. Section 14 of *Act 573* provides that the Director may, with the approval of the Minister, grant an indefinite residence status to a person who satisfies the Director that he is qualified under section 15 or 16 of that Act for that status. An application for an indefinite residence status shall be made to the Director using the prescribed form. A copy must be submitted to the Minister by the Director. The conditions to be complied with before a long-term residence is granted are provided for in section 15(1) of *Act 573*. A person qualifies for indefinite residence status if that person:

(a) has resided in Ghana throughout the period of twelve months immediately preceding the date of the application;
(b) has, during the seven years immediately preceding the period of the twelve months, resided in Ghana for an aggregated period amounting of at least five years;
(c) is of good character as attested to in writing by two Ghanaians who are notaries public, lawyers, senior public officers or any other class of persons approved of by the Minister;
(d) has not been sentenced to a period of imprisonment of twelve months or more;
(e) has made or is in the opinion of the Minister capable of making a substantial contribution to the development of Ghana;
(f) intends to reside permanently in Ghana upon the grant of the status; and
(g) possesses a valid residence permit on the date of his application.

141. *Act 573* makes provision for an adjustment in the years of residence that may entitle a person to an indefinite residence status. Section 15(2) of *Act 573* provides that the Director may, in special circumstances and with the approval of the Minister:

(a) *allow a continuous period of twelve months ending not more than six months before the date of application to be reckoned for purposes of Section 15(1)(a);*
(b) *allow periods of residence earlier than seven years before the date of application to be reckoned in computing the aggregate period mentioned in sub-section 1(b) of this section.*

Section 16(1) of *Act 573* provides for the issuing of an indefinite residence status to a foreign spouse as follows: a foreign spouse who wishes to be in Ghana indefinitely must submit an application and attach a marriage certificate to the application as evidence of qualifying as a spouse. Requirements in this case *include* proof of residence in Ghana during the period of twelve months immediately preceding the date of the application, residence in Ghana for an aggregated period of not less than two years, and possession of a valid residence permit on the date of the application.

II. Right of Abode

142. Section 17 of *Act 573* provides that the Minister may on application and with the approval of the President grant the status of right of abode to a Ghanaian by birth, adoption, registration or naturalization within the meaning of the *Citizenship Act* who, by reason of his acquisition of a foreign nationality, has lost his Ghanaian citizenship. The right of abode may also be granted to a person of African descent in the Diaspora. For a person of African descent in the Diaspora to be granted a right of abode status, the person must be of the minimum age of 18; of good character, and must have independent means and the ability to contribute substantially to national development. According to Regulation 13(2) of *L.I. 1691* a Ghanaian citizen who has lost his Ghanaian citizenship as stated in section 13(1)(a) of *L.I. 1691* must produce such documentary and other evidence to the Minister who may require testifying to the loss of his Ghanaian citizenship by reason of having acquired another citizenship which requires that he or she denounces his or her Ghanaian citizenship. Such an applicant shall not be required to produce documentary evidence of financial means.

143. A person of African descent in the Diaspora also qualifies to be considered for the status of a right of abode if he satisfies the Minister that he is of good character as attested to by two Ghanaians who are notaries public, lawyers, senior public officers or belong to another class of persons approved of by the Minister; has not been convicted of any criminal offence or sentenced to imprisonment for a term of twelve months or more; is of independent means or financial standing; is, in the opinion of the Minister, capable of making a substantial contribution to the development of Ghana; and has attained the age of 18 years. The High Court of Ghana, upon an application made by the Attorney-General, may deprive a person of the right of abode status if the activities of the holder are inimical to the security of the

State or prejudicial to public order, morality or public interest, or where the right was illegally or fraudulently acquired or if the holder no longer qualifies under the law.

§2. Administrative Procedures and Documents for Long-Term Residence

144. *Act 573* and *L.I. 1691* provide the required procedure and documents to make an indefinite residence and right of abode application. According to section 14 of *Act 573* entitled *Indefinite Residence Status*, the Director may with the approval of the Minister grant an indefinite residence status to a person who satisfies the Director that he qualifies for that status under section 15 or section 16 of that Act. An application for an indefinite residence status is made to the Director in the prescribed form who submits a copy to the Minister. Regulation 10 of *L.I. 1691* that provides for *Indefinite Residence Status* states that a foreign national who wishes to be considered for the granting of an indefinite residence status shall, in accordance with section 14 of the Act, submit an application to the Director using Form G in the Schedule to these Regulations. On receipt of the application, the Director must, after investigation, submit a recommendation to the Minister for consideration. Where an application is approved, the necessary endorsement is made in the passport of the applicant by the Director.

145. Section 17 of *Act 573* entitled *Right of Abode* provides that, subject to the section, the Minister may on application and with the approval of the President grant the status of right of abode to the qualified person in accordance with the provisions in Regulation 13 of *L.I. 1691*. The application for right of abode must be submitted by the application in person. Regulation 13 of *L.I. 1691* provides that the right of abode may be granted to a person of African descent in the Diaspora, if that person is at least aged 18, of good character, and has independent means and the ability to contribute substantially to the national development. A person of African descent in the Diaspora qualifies to be considered for the status of a right of abode if their immediate ancestors have resided outside the African Continent for at least three generations, but whose origin, either by documentary proof or by ethnic characteristics is African. According to Regulation 13(2) of *L.I. 1691*, a Ghanaian citizen who has lost his Ghanaian citizenship as stated in section 13(1)(a) of *L.I.1691* must present to the Minister such documentary and other evidence as required and the Minister may require testifying to the loss of his Ghanaian citizenship by reason of having acquired another citizenship.

§3. Legal Position of Long-Term Residents

146. Sections 18 and 19 of *Act 573* provide for the legal position of long-term residents, including the consequences, rights, and entitlements of being an indefinite resident and how such status can be lost. Section 18 is entitled *Consequences of Indefinite Residence Status and Right of Abode Status*. It provides that a person with an indefinite residence status or a person with a right of abode status (a) is entitled to remain indefinitely in Ghana; (b) is entitled to enter Ghana without a visa; and (c) is entitled to work in Ghana, either as self-employed person or as an employee without a work permit; (d) subject to the laws of Ghana.

147. Section 19 of *Act 573* provides for the revocation of the right of abode status by the High Court. It provides that the High Court may, on an application by the Attorney-General, deprive a person with a right of abode status of that status if the activities of that person are inimical to the security of the State or prejudicial to public order, public health, morality or public interest; or because the right was acquired by fraudulent misrepresentation, or any other illegal or irregular means; or that the holder of the status no longer qualifies under the law.

148. The *1992 Constitution* and *Immigration laws* of Ghana give long-term residents access to the rights generally enjoyed by Ghanaians. However, there are limitations and strict procedural processes in exercising the right to own real estate in Ghana, as Article 266(4) of Ghana's *Constitution* limits the right or interest that can be enjoyed in land or real estate in Ghana by a non-citizen, whether long-term resident or not, to leasehold for a term of not more than fifty years at any one time. Though such leases can be renewed repeatedly, Article 266(1) of the *Constitution* prohibits granting a freehold interest in any real estate in Ghana to non-citizens or foreigners. So a long-term resident can acquire real estate in Ghana on leasehold for a constitutionally specified renewable duration of fifty years at a time, but he or she cannot be vested with a freehold interest in or rights over any land in Ghana.

149. Long-term residents have the right to send their children to school, to pursue education at all levels, but they have to pay the fees prescribed for foreign students. They have the right of access to health service as well as any other utility and municipal service at the requisite fees or costs. On the right to work, section 18(1)(c) of *Act 573* stipulates that a long-term resident with an indefinite residence status or a right of abode status is entitled to work in Ghana without a work permit either as self-employed person or as an employee. However, the *Ghana Investment Promotion Act, 2013 (Act 865)* reserves some businesses for Ghanaians exclusively and provides for minimum foreign capital investment requirements for enterprises in which foreign participation is permitted (*see* paragraphs 40 and 41 *supra*).

§4. Position of Family Members

I. Dependency Permit

150. Act 573 provides a right of residence for dependents of a holder of an indefinite residence or a right of abode status. The Act defines a dependent to include a child and a spouse. According to section 18(2) of *Act 573* a child and other dependents of a person with an/ indefinite residence status or right of abode status are eligible for a *dependency permit* subject to the conditions as specified in the dependency permit. The Act defines a child to mean a natural or adopted child under the age of 18 years. Section 18(2) of *Act 573* provides as follows: 'A non-Ghanaian child or any other non-Ghanaian dependant of a person with (a) indefinite residence status or (b) right of abode status, is eligible for a dependency permit'. A *dependency permit* may on an application be issued by the Director and shall be subject to the conditions specified in the permit.

II. Indefinite Residence for Foreign Spouse

151. Section 16 of *Act 573* and Regulation 11 of *L.I. 1691* provide for the right to indefinite residence of a foreign spouse. A 'foreign spouse' means a foreign national married to a Ghanaian citizen and, a 'foreign national' means a person who is not a citizen of Ghana. A foreign spouse who wishes to remain in Ghana indefinitely must submit an application for this purpose and shall attach to the application a marriage certificate as evidence of being a spouse and satisfy the conditions listed in section 16(1) of the Act, namely that the foreign spouse:

(a) has resided in Ghana throughout the period of twelve months immediately preceding the date of the application;
(b) has immediately preceding the period of the twelve months, resided in Ghana for an aggregate period of no less than two years;
(c) has not been convicted for any offence and sentenced to a period of imprisonment of twelve months or more;
(d) intends to reside permanently in Ghana upon the grant of the status; and
(e) is in possession of a valid residence permit on the date of the application.

152. Section 16 of *Act 573* provides other detailed rules on indefinite residence for foreign spouses including adjustments in the years of residence that may qualify a foreign spouse for an indefinite residence status, the loss of that status, reinstatement of that status, and the implications of a separation, divorce or death of spouse for that status as follows:

(2) *The Director may in such special circumstances as he thinks fit and with the approval of the Minister allow a continuous period of six months and an aggregate period of one year to be substituted for the twelve months and two years respectively provided under paragraphs (a) and (b) of subsection (1).*
(3) *Where a foreign spouse who is granted an indefinite residence status leaves Ghana for more than twelve consecutive months that foreign spouse automatically loses the status.*
(4) *A foreign spouse who loses an indefinite residence status under subsection (3) may apply to the Director for reinstatement, subject to the condition that the application shall be treated as a fresh application subject to such conditions as the Director may determine.*
(5) *The separation, divorce or death of a spouse in a marriage to which this section applies shall not affect the indefinite residence status held by the foreign spouse immediately before the occurrence of the event.*

(6) *Notwithstanding any provision of this section, a foreign spouse whose marriage is no longer in existence may upon application to the Director be granted indefinite residence status subject to evidence that the marriage was contracted in good faith.*

Part III. Right of Residence for Specific Categories of Persons

Chapter 1. Nationals with Preferential Treatment

153. Ghana does not have a specific policy on preferential treatment for the citizens or nationals of any country on refugee and asylum matters. However, section 3(4) of the *Immigration Act, 2000 (Act 573)* provides for free movement across the border by a border-resident residing within a 5 kilometre radius of either side of Ghana's territorial frontiers with the Republics of Togo, Burkina Faso and Cote d'Ivoire for the purpose of attending to his or her routine economic or social matters. Thus given Ghana's proximity to neighbours such as Cote d'Ivoire, Burkina Faso, Togo, and other countries in the ECOWAS sub-region such as Benin, Nigeria, Mali, Niger, Sierra Leone, Liberia, Gambia, Guinea, etc., as well as its obligations under the *ECOWAS Treaty* of 1975, and the *Revised ECOWAS Treaty of 1997*, it seems that Ghana is obliged politically and legally to give preferential treatment to ECOWAS nationals. Article 3(1) of the *Revised ECOWAS Treaty of 1997* insists on '[t]he removal, between Member States, of obstacles to the free movement of persons, goods, services and capital, and to the right of residence and establishment'. Moreover, the OAU (now AU) *Convention Governing the Specific Aspects of Refugee Problems in Africa* allows for the *group-based determination of refugee status.* It defines 'refugee' to include every person compelled to flee 'external aggression, occupation, foreign domination or events seriously disturbing public order in either part or the whole of his country of origin or nationality'. Thus large groups of refugees can be given protection on the strength of their nationality or membership of a particular ethnic group. This expanded definition of refugee benefits AU States parties to the *Convention Governing the Specific Aspects of Refugee Problems in Africa,* and may be deemed preferential treatment.

Chapter 2. Students

154. To study in Ghana, the prospective student should have an offer of admission from a recognized and accredited education institution in Ghana. Students who are not from ECOWAS States are required to obtain visa or entry permits before proceeding to Ghana. Students are usually issued F-1 or F-2 visa. The following requirements should be met irrespective of the nationality of a prospective student before the issuance of a residence permit:

- enter with a valid travel document (i.e., passport, ECOWAS Travel Document);
- provide evidence of an admission letter from an accredited tertiary institution;
- have an offer of approved course from an accredited institution;
- submit proof of exemption or payment of a course fee;
- have a guarantee of accommodation;
- provide evidence of financial support;
- have paid the prescribed fees for the residence permit; and
- Have completed an application form which is submitted with the specified number of passport size photographs.

155. Although students are not specifically mentioned in the main immigration laws such as Act 573 and *L.I. 1691*, there are administrative instructions and practices that regulate their entry into Ghana. Section 13 of Act 573 and *Regulation 9 of L.I.1691* allow the Director of Immigration to grant a residence permit to a foreign national who intends to remain in Ghana for a substantial period, and for a student, such a permit is granted for the duration of the approved course offered him by the accredited institution. Under section 13(2) of *Act 573*, the Director may grant a residence permit for up to a period not exceeding eight years, and a residence permit shall not be for more than four years in first instance. As prescribed by Regulation 9 of *L.I. 1691*, a residence permit is granted subject to the condition that the person to whom it is granted shall not undertake any employment or engage in any business, trade or profession except as may be specified in the permit. A student may therefore not embark on any business or take up a profession unless specified in the permit.

156. When a residence permit expires, Regulation 9 of *L.I. 1691* provides for its extension as follows: 'a person granted four years residence permit in the first instance may subsequently apply for an extension of the residence permit for a further period. The Director may, if satisfied that the person has fulfilled all the conditions subject to which the previous permit was granted, and has not abused any privilege granted that person under the previous permit, grant such a person an extension of the permit for a period not exceeding four years.' Students seeking renewal of their residence permit are to attach a letter of application from the school to their completed application form that is accompanied with the specified number of passport size photographs.

Chapter 3. Researchers

157. Although researchers are not specifically mentioned in the main immigration laws such as *Act 573* and *L.I. 1691*, there are administrative instructions and practices that regulate their entry into Ghana. Depending on the proposed length of stay of a researcher in Ghana, a *transit visa, visitor's visa or a residence permit* may be issued to the researcher. The requirements and conditions for the grant of such visa or permits apply to the researcher subject to the necessary modifications. Regulation 8(1) and 8(2) of *L.I. 1691* provide that: 'in any situation where a transit visa, a residence permit, an indefinite residence or a right of abode status … is inapplicable, the immigration officer may grant a visitor's visa. A visitor's visa shall be subject to the condition that the person to whom it is granted shall not undertake or follow any occupation for reward, except such as may be specified in the visa'. A visitor's visa shall be for a period determined by the immigration officer, but shall not exceed two months or in the case of a national of an ECOWAS country three months as provided in the ECOWAS Treaty. Extensions to the initial sixty or ninety days visitors permit may be granted on application to the Director in the prescribed manner for a renewal of the permit within one month before the permit expires (*section 23 of Act 573*).The GIS may extend such permits up to a minimum of three months initially and a maximum of six months. In applying for extension or stay, the researcher visitor will have to:

- complete the requisite application forms obtained from the Immigration Headquarters or the nearest Regional Command of the Service;
- provide two current passport-sized photographs;
- write an application letter stating reason (s) for the request (i.e., visitors who wish to stay for a period more than three months);
- provide a valid return ticket or any form of guarantee that the visitor will leave the country at the end of the period requested for;
- provide a valid passport; and
- pay the requisite processing fee and the prescribed fees for residence permit.

Applications for an extension attract a monthly fee for dependents, Ghanaians with foreign passports, ECOWAS nationals or other non-nationals.

158. Any person other than a prohibited immigrant affected by a refusal to grant or renew a permit or a revocation of a permit under Act 573 by an immigration officer may submit a petition to the Minister within seven days of such action. The Minister shall, subject to the prescribed procedure, take such action as he considers appropriate (section 46 of *Act 573*).According to section 47 of *Act 573*, a petition to the Minister under section 46 does not a stay the action which has been petitioned against. There are, however, regulations that provide conditions under which a person may be permitted to stay in Ghana pending the hearing of a petition made by that person.

Chapter 4. Labour and Economic Migration

§1. Labour Employment

159. There are several legislative acts on labour employment migration in Ghana. Most of the rules are discussed in-depth in Part VII. Suffice it to say that the *Immigration Act, 2000 (Act 573*), the *Immigration Regulations, 2001(L.I. 1697*), the *GIPC Act, 2013* (*Act 865*), the *Free Zones Act, 1995 (Act 504*), the *Labour Act, 2003 (Act 651*), the *Labour Regulations, 2007 (L.I. 1833)*, regulate migrant labour employment. The main legislation on this subject is the *Immigration Act, 2000 (Act 573)* which has provisions in sections 24–34 on the employment of foreign nationals in accordance with an immigrant quota administered by the Immigrant Quota Committee. It also provides for the calculation of the immigrant quota, work permits for foreign immigrants, guarantees and obligations of both the employer and the foreign employee. As a rule, a foreign national cannot be employed in Ghana except in accordance with a permit granted by the Immigrant Quota Committee.

§2. Seasonal Workers and Temporary Workers

160. Ghana grants H1–H4 visas to temporary workers. But the key migration laws in Ghana such as *Act 573* and *L.I.1691* do not make explicit provisions for temporary workers. The expression 'temporary workers' is not even mentioned in those laws. However the *Labour Act, 2003 (Act 651)* has provisions on it. According to section 78 of *Act 651*, 'a "temporary worker" means a worker who is employed for a continuous period of not less than one month and is not a permanent worker or employed for a work that is seasonal in character.' 'Temporary worker' as defined in the *Labour Act, 2003 (Act 651)* is mainly for purposes of the provisions relating to temporary workers in that Act. That notwithstanding, Ghana's migration rules, procedures and practices recognize temporary workers and permit them to enter Ghana on H1–H4 visas to work in the country for the duration of the visa.

161. Section 24 of *Act 573* also makes provision for employment of foreign nationals. Subject to the Act, a person shall not employ a foreign national in Ghana except in accordance with a permit granted by the Immigrant Quota Committee established under section 25. Regulation 16 of *L.I.1691* also stipulates that an employer who wishes to apply for a work permit for a person employed by that employer shall submit an application through the Director, who upon investigation shall submit a report to the Immigrant Quota Committee for consideration and approval. A permit to employ a foreign national shall be as in *Form L* in the Schedule.

§3. Independent Economic Activities

162. There are several rules on independent economic migration in Ghana. Part VIII provides an in-depth discussion. Section 18(1)(c) of Immigration Act, 2000

(Act 573) provides that 'a person with indefinite residence status or a person with right of abode status is entitled to work in Ghana as self-employed or as an employee without a work permit'. Section 27(3) of 573 further provides that the Minister may issue a work permit to a person who is not a prohibited immigrant, (nor a visitor, tourist, transit passenger or student) and who satisfies the Immigrant Quota Committee that he wishes to enter Ghana in order to take up work or employment; is qualified to work or undertake employment in the trade, business or calling in respect of which the application is made; the taking up of the work or employment will be to the benefit generally of Ghana; and is lawfully resident in Ghana and is qualified to work as an employee or be self-employed.

163. Self-employed enterprises of foreign immigrants are often governed by the Immigration Act, Companies Code, GIPC Act, 2013 (Act 865), Free Zones Act, 1995 (Act 504) among others. Under section 27 of *Act 865*, certain activities are exclusively reserved for Ghanaians (*see* paragraph 40 *supra*). The Free Zones Act, 1995 (Act 504) also deals with promoting investment, especially in the manufacturing sector, with the aim of exporting the bulk of the products and provides several rules for the participation of foreign investors in Free Zones.

164. Article 18 of the UN Convention Relating to the Status of Refugees as incorporated into the Refugees Act of Ghana also recognizes the right of refugees to self-employment and requires Contracting States to 'accord to a refugee lawfully in their territory treatment as favourable as possible and, in any event not less favourable than that accorded to aliens generally in the same circumstances, as regards the right to engage on his own account in agriculture, industry, handicrafts and commerce and to establish commercial and industrial companies'.

Section 6 of the Internal Revenue (Registration of Business) Act, 2005 (Act 684) provides categories of self-employed persons for purposes of fees for registration of the business. The Commissioner of Internal Revenue may determine categories of business of self-employed persons and the registration fees payable by the categories, and resolve, if there is doubt,whether a business falls into one category or the other. These categories are also relevant for the payment of taxes (Internal Revenue Act, 2000 (Act 592), Income Tax (Standard Assessments) Instrument, 1974 (L.I. 974), etc.).

165. Section 45 of the Social Security Act, 1991 (PNDCL 247) defines a 'self-employed person' as a person who does not have any other employer and works on that person's own account. Section 20(1)(c) of the Social Security Act, 1991 (PNDCL 247) provides that the Act applies to all self-employed persons, who opt to join the scheme. Since the Act does not explicitly exclude foreigners, it applies to a self-employed foreigner who opts to join the scheme. Where a member has ceased to be employed, the member may continue to pay the monthly contribution at the rate being paid by a self-employed person (section 20(2) of PNDCL 247). Section 22(4) of that law provides that the rate of contribution of a self-employed person shall be 17.5% of any income for the month from the profession, vocation, business or occupation of that person. The Social Security Act has been revised by the Social Security Act, 2009 (Act 766) which pegs the monthly contributions of self-employed persons at 13.5%. Thus, with effect from 2010, those who opt to join the Scheme as 'Voluntary Contributors' under Act 766 have to pay 13.5% rate while those under PNDCL 247 have to pay 17.5%.

§4. Investment Activities

166. The rules on investment migration in Ghana are contained in the Immigration Act, 2000 (Act 573), Immigration Regulations, 2001 (L.I. 1697), GIPC Act, 2013 (Act 865), Free Zones Act, 1995 (Act 504), Minerals and Mining Act 2006 (Act 703), Internal Revenue Act, 2000 (Act 592) as amended, Labour Act 2003 (Act 651), Labour Regulations, 2007 (L.I. 1833) among several other laws.

167. Migrants and foreigners can invest in all other sectors in Ghana including mining, real estate, agriculture, ICT, manufacturing, education, construction, hospitality, etc., with the exception of activities prohibited for foreigners and reserved for Ghanaians only as discussed *supra* in paragraph 40. Section 28 of *Act 865* prescribes minimum foreign capital investment in Ghana for enterprise in which foreign participation is permitted as highlighted *supra* in paragraph 41. *Act 865* also provides for varying immigrant quotas based on a foreign enterprise's paid-up capital. Paragraph 42 *supra* discusses these *quotas* in detail.

168. The Free Zones Act, 1995 (Act 504) also deals with promoting investment, especially in the manufacturing sector, with the aim of exporting the bulk of the products, and provides several rules for the participation of foreign investors in Free Zones.

Chapter 5. Humanitarian Reasons

§1. Humanitarian or Compassionate Grounds

169. Ghana may grant residence permit on humanitarian or compassionate grounds under section 51(b) of the Immigration Act, 2000 (Act 573). It falls under the Residual Powers given to the Minister. Consequently, notwithstanding anything to the contrary in the Immigration Act, the Minister may revoke or waive any visa, permit, conditions of entry and any requirement on grounds of (a) national interest, (b) compassionate circumstances; or (c) any other reasonable ground. Even though the word humanitarian is not used in the act, 'compassionate circumstances' is expressly stated as a basis upon which the residual powers of the Minister may be triggered. It is therefore possible for persons, including those who are seriously ill, and pregnant women, to be given permits, visa, or other conditions of entry into Ghana on compassionate or humanitarian grounds. The Act also adds a very broad scoped 'any other reasonable ground' as a basis upon which permits may be granted or revoked.

§2. Unaccompanied Minor Children

170. Ghana's immigration and refugee laws do not deal with the issue of non-accompanied minors. However, various laws and regulatory procedures may apply to such persons. Under Ghana's laws, such as Regulation 42 of the *National Vocational Training Board (Apprentice Training) Regulations, 1978 (L.I. 1151)*, a minor is a person below 21 years old. Section 1 of the Children's Act, 1998 (Act 560), also defines a child as a person under 18 years of age. A 'young person' is above 18 years, but under 21 years (section 124 of Act 560). Thus a minor who falls in the under 18 age range is a child but a minor in the 'young person' range is not a child under Ghana's laws and as such may not benefit from many of the laws that protect children in Ghana. Such a minor or 'young person' will nevertheless be protected under laws governing minors. If a non-accompanied minor is below 18 years, he or she may benefit from the *Children's Act, 1998 Act 560, Child Rights Regulations, 2002 (L.I.1705), Human Trafficking Act, 2005 (Act 694), Citizenship Act, 2000 (Act 591), Labour Act, 2000 (Act 651),Labour Regulations, 2007 (L.I. 1833)*, etc. For instance, section 3 of *Act 560* provides that '*a person shall not discriminate against a child* on the grounds of gender, race, age, religion, disability, health status, custom, ethnic origin, rural or urban background, birth or *any other status*, socio-economic status or *because the child is a refugee*'. Section 18 of Act 560 further provides care and protection for any child who is an orphan or is deserted by the relatives, is destitute, is wandering and does not have a home or settled place of abode or visible means of subsistence, or is otherwise exposed to moral or physical danger. Section 18 also covers any child who has been neglected or ill-treated by the person who has the care and custody of the child, is begging or receiving alms, or is found in a street, premises or a place for the purpose of begging or receiving alms, or accompanies a person when that person is begging or receiving alms.

171. Section 16(1) of the Children's Act, 1998, Act 560 provides that 'a District Assembly shall protect the welfare and promote the rights of children within its area of authority and shall ensure that within the district, governmental agencies liaise with each other in matters concerning children'. Thus, the Social Welfare and Community Development Department of every District Assembly has been tasked with the responsibility to investigate every case where it has reasonable grounds to suspect that a child is in need of care and protection. If it is determined that the child is in need of immediate care and protection, the Department shall direct a probation officer or social welfare officer accompanied by the police to remove the child to a place of safety for a period of not more than seven days. The child shall be brought before a family tribunal by the probation officer or social welfare officer before the expiry of the seven-day period for care order to be made. Until the family tribunal determines the order, the family tribunal may commit the child to an approved residential home or to the care of a probation officer, social welfare officer or any other suitable person.

Investigation by Department

172. Under the *Children's Act, 1998 (Act 560)*as amended by the *Children's (Amendment) Act, 2016 (Act 937)* where the Department has reasonable grounds to suspect that a child is being abused, or needs care and protection, it shall direct a probation or social welfare officer accompanied by a police officer to enter the premises where the child resides to investigate, or to refer the matter to a child panel if the child is not in immediate need of care and protection. If the investigation determines that the child has been abused he shall be removed to the home of a parent, guardian or approved relative or placed with a fit person at the direction of the Department of Social Welfare in the district for maximum period of seven days. The child shall be brought before a family tribunal before the expiry of the seven-day period for a care order to be made. After the seven days, but before the family tribunal determines the order, the child may be placed in an approved residential home, in the care of a probation officer, social welfare officer or with another fit person.[92]

Care Order of Family Tribunal

173. Also, upon application by a probation or social welfare officer, a family tribunal may make a care order removing a child from a harmful or potentially harmful situation and transfer parental rights to the Department. The child may be placed with a fit person, or at the home of a parent, guardian or approved relative. The decision of the Department to place the child with any of these persons may be confirmed or varied by the regional Foster Care Placement Committee. The care order stays in effect for three years or until the child turns eighteen, whichever occurs first. The family tribunal may also make an order for the financial maintenance of the child by the person responsible for the child. The manager of an institution can be

92. *See* s. 19 of the Children's Act, 1998 (Act 560) as amended by s. 2 of the Children's (Amendment) Act, 2016 (Act 937).

an approved fit person for the care of a child only if the institution in question has been approved by notice published in the Gazette by the Minister for Social Welfare, or if the institution has been assigned that function by an Act of Parliament.[93]

Supervision Order of Family Tribunal

174. Upon application by a probation or social welfare officer, a family tribunal may issue a supervision order to prevent harm to a child in the custody of a parent, guardian or relative. The probation or social welfare officer shall supervise the parent, guardian or relative's care of the child. The supervision order stays in effect for one year or until the child turns eighteen, whichever occurs first.[94]

Duties of Probation Officer and Social Worker

175. When a care or supervision order is made, the probation or social welfare officer must advise the child and family, take reasonable steps to ensure that the child does not come to any harm and should hold regular interviews to help plan for the child's future.[95]

Home Visits

176. A probation officer or social welfare officer shall be permitted by a parent, guardian or relative of the child to visit the child at the family home.[96]

General Provisions on Orders

177. A child who flouts a family tribunal's order and runs away from the place of care or supervision may be arrested by the police and returned to the place of safety. If the approved fit person is not willing to take the child back, the tribunal may order the child placed elsewhere.[97]

Discharge of Orders

178. A care or supervision order may be discharged in the best interest of the child by the family tribunal upon the application made by the child, the probation or social welfare officer, the parent, the guardian or a relative.[98]

Care Order and Adoption

93. *See* s. 20 of the Children's Act, 1998 (Act 560) as amended by s. 3 of Act 937.
94. *See* s. 21 of the Children's Act, 1998 (Act 560).
95. *See* s. 22 of the Children's Act, 1998 (Act 560).
96. *See* s. 23 of the Children's Act, 1998 (Act 560).
97. *See* s. 24 of the Children's Act, 1998 (Act 560).
98. *See* s. 25 of the Children's Act, 1998 (Act 560).

179. If a child is placed under a care order and the parent, guardian or relative of the child shows no interest in the child's welfare within the period stipulated by a family tribunal, the child may be put up for adoption.[99]

The Citizenship Act, 2000 (Act 591) also has relevant provisions that can apply to non-accompanied minors. Section 9 of Act 591 provides that '*a child of not more than sixteen years of age neither of whose parents is a citizen who is adopted by a citizen becomes by virtue of the adoption, a citizen of Ghana*'. Section 8 of Act 591 also provides that, '*a child of not more than seven years of age found in Ghana whose parents are not known shall be presumed to be a citizen by birth*'. Though this provision deals with foundlings, and is a rebuttable presumption, it can nevertheless be applied to a non-accompanied minor depending on the situation.

§3. Victims of Trafficking in Human Beings

180. Ghana has laws that provide measures to protect victims of human trafficking. The *Human Trafficking Act, 2005 (Act 694)* provides rules to prevent, combat and punish the trafficking in persons. Chapter 5 of Ghana's *1992 Constitution* safeguards fundamental human rights and freedoms including right of movement, entry into Ghana, personal liberty and dignity of the person. It also prohibits torture, inhuman or degrading treatment, slavery, servitude, and forced labour. According to section 1 of the *Human Trafficking Act, 2005 (Act 694)*, human trafficking is the recruiting, transporting, transferring, harbouring or trading persons within and across national borders using threats, force, fraud, abuse of power, exploitation or financial incentive. Exploitation includes sexual exploitation, such as induced prostitution, forced labour, slavery and the removal of organs. Trafficking includes placement for sale, bonded or temporary placement, or placement where exploitation by someone else is the motivating factor. Where children are trafficked, neither the consent of the child nor its parents or guardian can be used as a defence in prosecution even if the trafficker used fraud or deception, abuse of power, or took advantage of the vulnerability of the child.[100]

Filing of Complaint to Police

181. A complaint may be filed by a victim of trafficking or someone with information, where the victim or the offender resides, where the trafficking occurred, or where the victim is residing temporarily. A social welfare officer, probation officer, health care provider, teacher, district labour officer may also file a complaint where intervention is in the best interest of the victim. A child may be assisted by a next friend to file a complaint. Where a victim is for any reason unable to file a complaint, a member of his family or any person with knowledge of the offence may file on the victim's behalf. If the victim is deceased, the next-of-kin or any person with knowledge of the offence may file a complaint.[101]

---

99. *See* s. 26 of the Children's Act, 1998 (Act 560).
100. *See* s. 1 of the Human Trafficking Act, 2005 (Act 694).
101. *See* s. 9 of the Human Trafficking Act, 2005 (Act 694).

Police Assistance, Receipt of Complaint by Police and Rescue of Trafficked Persons

182. A police officer shall respond and offer protection when trafficking is alleged even if the person making the report is not the victim. Failure to respond shall subject the police officer to Police Service disciplinary procedure if a report is filed with his superior officer.[102] Upon receiving a complaint, the police officer shall take a detailed statement from the parties and witnesses and provide a copy to the victim, get the victim medical treatment and a place of safety where necessary and inform the victim of his/her rights and of any available material support. A next friend shall be present when the statement is being taken from a child.[103] An authorized officer in collaboration with an Organization, or any government agency can rescue a trafficked person.[104]

Temporary Care and Counselling of Trafficked Person

183. Temporary basic material support and counselling services shall be provided by the Ministry through the District Assembly with resources from the Fund. The District Assembly shall consult in these matters with the relevant government agencies and organizations within its area of authority.[105]

Non-deportation of Victims of Human Trafficking

184. Human Trafficking Act, 2005 (Act 694) protects victims of human trafficking, by making an exception to the 'removal of an illegal immigrant' provisions in section 21 of the Immigration Act, 2000 (Act 573). Under section 21, where the presence of a person in Ghana is unlawful, that person may be repatriated from Ghana by an order of the Director. But section 34(1) of the *Human Trafficking Act, 2005 (Act 694)*, provides that, despite the provisions in section 21 of the Immigration Act, 2000 (Act 573), a trafficked person who is in Ghana unlawfully, may remain in Ghana throughout the period of a legal investigation and prosecution of a trafficker. The Human Trafficking Management Board shall, in such cases, make arrangements for the repatriation of the trafficked person upon completion of the legal process, but shall stay in a reception centre provided by the Ministry of Interior where basic material support shall be provided until the repatriation. However, if it is in the best interest of the trafficked person, then he or she may be allowed to remain in Ghana after the legal process with approval of Minister of Interior and the person shall stay in a shelter provided by the Ministry where the person shall receive basic material support until resettled in Ghana.[106]

Compensation

102. *See* s. 10 of the Human Trafficking Act, 2005 (Act 694).
103. *See* s. 11 of the Human Trafficking Act, 2005 (Act 694).
104. *See* s. 14 of the Human Trafficking Act, 2005 (Act 694).
105. *See* ss 15 &16 of the Human Trafficking Act, 2005 (Act 694).
106. *See* s. 34(2) of the Human Trafficking Act, 2005 (Act 694).

185. A person convicted of trafficking shall be ordered to pay compensation to the trafficking victim. A person who causes injury to another during trafficking shall be ordered to pay compensation to the injured person. The payment of compensation shall be in addition to any other punishment.[107]

The Human Trafficking Fund

186. A Human Trafficking Fund has been established pursuant to the *Human Trafficking Act, 2005 (Act 694)*. It consists of voluntary contributions from individuals and Organizations, money approved by Parliament, grants from bilateral and multilateral sources, the proceeds from the confiscation of property connected with trafficking, and any other moneys approved by the Minister for Finance. The Fund shall be applied toward the basic material support, skills training, family tracing, rescue, rehabilitation, reintegration and construction of reception shelters for trafficking victims. Persons connected with rescue, rehabilitation and reintegration shall also receive training and capacity building from the Fund.[108]

Tracing of Family of Trafficked Person

187. The Ministry shall be assisted by the police, an Organization or any other person with information to trace the family of a trafficked person and shall consider the views of the trafficked person regarding reunification with his/her family. [109]

Rehabilitation of Trafficked Person

188. The Ministry shall help to provide a rescued trafficking victim with employable skills, employment opportunities or start-up capital. The Fund may also provide financial assistance to trafficking victims. Rescue, rehabilitation and reintegration of a trafficked child shall be performed with a view to the best interest of the child.[110]

189. *The Immigration (Amendment) Act, 2012 (Act 848)* also amended the *Immigration Act, 2000 (Act 573)* to provide for the offence of migrant smuggling. *Act 848* inserted section 52A entitled 'Prohibition of migrant smuggling' into *Act 573*. Section 52A of *Act 573* and *Act 848* provides that a person shall not engage in migrant smuggling. A person who engages in migrant smuggling commits an offence and is liable on conviction to a fine of not less than 625 penalty units and not more than 1,250 penalty units or to a term of imprisonment of not less than five years and not more than ten years or to both.

190. Migrant smuggling is defined in section 52A to mean 'the facilitation of the unlawful entry or departure from the country of a person in order to obtain, directly

107. *See* s. 19 of the Human Trafficking Act, 2005 (Act 694).
108. *See* ss 20–22 of the Human Trafficking Act, 2005 (Act 694).
109. *See* s. 17 of the Human Trafficking Act, 2005 (Act 694).
110. *See* s. 18 of the Human Trafficking Act, 2005 (Act 694).

or indirectly, a financial or other material benefit'. 'Facilitation' is also described in section 52A to include '*(a)* producing, procuring, providing or processing a travel or identity document by fraudulent means; *(b)* procuring by unlawful means other documentation in support of the processing of a travel or identity document; and *(c)* enabling a person who is not a national or a permanent resident to remain in the country without complying with the requirement for legally remaining in the country by any of the means mentioned in paragraphs*(a)* and *(b)*'.

§4. Others

191. Other humanitarian statuses that exist in Ghana include asylum seeker and refugee. These would however be treated in the immediately ensuing paragraphs of Chapter 6 *infra*.

Chapter 6. Asylum

§1. Conditions

192. When people flee from their own country and seek sanctuary in another country, they apply for asylum, and may eventually be granted refugee status after due processes and procedures. Asylum is thus a right accorded a refugee to enable him receive legal protection and material assistance. Recognizing the social and humanitarian nature of the problem of refugees, Ghana has ratified several international laws and conventions relating to refugees, including the *1951 UN Convention relating to the status of Refugees*, the *1967 UN Protocol Relating to the status of Refugees*, and the *1969 OAU Convention Governing the Specific Aspects of Refugee Problems in Africa*. All of these conventions are mentioned in section 11 of Ghana's Refugee Law, 1992 (PNDCL 305D) and their contents are fully reproduced in the Schedule to that law.

193. According to section 56 of the Immigration Act, 2000 (Act 573), a 'refugee' means a person who, owing to well-founded fear of being persecuted for reasons of race, religion, nationality, membership of a particular social group or political opinion, is outside the country of his nationality and is unable or unwilling to avail himself of the protection of that country, or who not having a nationality and being outside the country of his former habitual residence is, owing to such fear unable or unwilling to return to it, or who owing to external aggression, occupation, foreign domination or events seriously disturbing public order in either part or the whole of his country of origin or nationality, is compelled to seek refuge in another place outside his country; or any person stipulated by the Government to belong to this class. This definition seems to summarize the definition for refugees in the international conventions that Ghana has ratified.

194. Under the 1951 United Nations Convention Relating to the Status of Refugees and the United Nations Protocol Relating to the Status of Refugees of 1967 to which Ghana is a signatory:

> a refugee is someone who owing to well-founded fear of being persecuted for reasons of race, religion, nationality, membership of a particular social group or political opinion, is outside the country of his nationality and is unable or, owing to such fear, is unwilling to avail himself of the protection of that country; or who, not having a nationality and being outside the country of his former habitual residence as a result of such events, is unable or, owing to such fear, is unwilling to return to it.

195. Also, the erstwhile *Organisation of Africa Unity* (now African Union) *Convention Governing the Specific Aspects of Refugee Problems in Africa of 1969*, which Ghana has ratified extends further the definition of a refugee to mean:

> every person who, owing to well-founded fear of being persecuted for reasons of race, religion, nationality, membership of a particular social group or politi

cal opinion, is outside the country of his nationality and is unable or, owing to such fear, is unwilling to avail himself of the protection of that country, or who, not having a nationality and being outside the country of his former habitual residence as a result of such events is unable or owing to such fear, is unwilling to return to it.

196. According to the *Organisation of Africa Unity* (now African Union) *Convention Governing the Specific Aspects of Refugee Problems in Africa of 1969*, the term refugee shall also apply to 'every person who owing to external aggression, occupation, foreign domination or events seriously disturbing public order in either part or the whole of his country of origin or nationality, is compelled to leave his place of habitual residence in order to seek refuge in another place outside his country of origin or nationality'.

197. Persons fleeing war zones, persecution or persons from refugee producing countries do not necessarily require travel documents to enter Ghana. It is generally accepted if such persons enter through either an approved or an unapproved route. Therefore section 2 of the Refugees Law, 1992 (PNDCL 305D) which is headed, illegal entry or presence in Ghana of a refugee provides as follows:

> notwithstanding any provision of the Aliens Act, 1963 (Act 160) [now *Immigration Act, 2000 (Act 573)*] but subject to the provisions of this Law, a person claiming to be a refugee within the meaning of this Law, who illegally enters Ghana or is illegally present in Ghana shall not be declared a prohibited immigrant; be detained; or be imprisoned or penalised in any other manner merely by reason of his illegal entry or presence pending the determination of his application for a refugee status.

§2. PROCEDURES

198. An asylum seeker who enters Ghana has to present him/herself to Immigration Officers at the point of entry and declare the intention of seeking asylum in Ghana. Where an asylum seeker enters the country without passing through an approved route, he is required by law to present himself to the nearest immigration office or UNHCR office within fourteen days. An asylum seeker who cannot speak or write English is usually provided with an interpreter by UNHCR. An asylum seeker is required to fill an Initial Registration Form (IRF). The applicant will be forwarded to GRB. The asylum seeker will thereafter be given an appointment for Refugee Status Determination. Asylum seeker having any form of identification is required to bring it to the interview. An asylum seeker who has applied for recognition as a refugee and each of his members has the right to remain within Ghana, pending the decision of his application from GRB. The decision of GRB will be communicated to the asylum seeker in writing as to whether his/her claim as a refugee has been accepted or refused. Where an asylum seeker's application to be recognized as a refugee is refused, he can appeal against the decision within thirty days upon receiving the decision.

199. In accordance with the provisions of section 8 of the Refugee Law, 1992 (PNDCL 305D), the Director upon the recommendation of the Refugee Board shall issue any relevant immigrant document in respect of a refugee in Ghana. PNDCL 305D provides details on the procedure for application, grant, withdrawal and cessation of refugee status as follows:

Application for Refugee Status

200. A person who is within the boundaries of Ghana, whether he entered lawfully or not, and who wishes to stay in Ghana as a refugee shall within fourteen days of such entry apply to the Ghana Refuge Board for recognition of his refugee status. This can be done at the point of entry, through any immigration officer or police officer or through the office of the UNHCR in Ghana. This application shall be forwarded to the Board within seven days of receipt. The Board has thirty days to consider the application, during which period it may make enquiries or invite the applicant before it. After the investigation, the Board shall notify the applicant in writing of its decision to grant or deny the application.[111]

201. Section 9 of PNDCL 305D deals with appeal on refusal to be granted refugee status and provides that when an application for refugee status is denied, the applicant may, within thirty days of notification of such denial, appeal in writing to the Secretary, who may confirm or reverse the decision of the Board and notify the applicant in writing. This decision of the Secretary is final. In considering the appeal, the Secretary may invite the UNHCR representative in Ghana to make oral or written representation in the matter, refer the matter back to the Board for further inquiry, or make such further inquiry and investigation into the matter as he thinks necessary. The applicant can stay in the country during the appeal period.

202. Section 10 of PNDCL 305D entitled residence in the Republic pending recognition, provides that despite the provisions of any other law, a person who has applied for recognition as a refugee, and each member of that person's family shall have the right to remain within the Republic until that person has been recognized as a refugee. In the event of the application being unsuccessful, the applicant and each member of that his family shall have the right to remain within the Republic until the applicant has had the opportunity to exhaust the right of appeal under section 9. Where an appeal has been dismissed, the applicant and each member of his family shall have the right to remain within the Republic until the applicant has been allowed a reasonable time not exceeding three months, to seek admission to a country of the his choice. The three months may however be extended by the Minister where on an application made to the Minister by the person concerned, the Minister is satisfied that there is a reasonable likelihood of that person being admitted to a country of that person's choice within the extended period.

203. The provisions of section 15 of PNDCL305D details the instances where the grant of refugee status to a person seeking refuge in Ghana may be withdrawn.

111. Section 8 of the Refugee Law, 1992 (PNDCL 305D).

They indicate that where the Board is of the opinion that a refugee should not have been accorded refugee status or no longer qualifies as a refugee, they may withdraw that person's refugee status and notify the refugee in writing. A refugee, upon being notified of this withdrawal of status has fourteen days to appeal in writing to the Secretary. The decision of the Secretary is final. the Secretary may invite the UNHCR representative in Ghana to make oral or written representation in the matter, refer the matter back to the Board for further investigation, or make such further inquiry and investigation into the matter as he thinks necessary.

204. Section 16 of PNDCL 305D, provides the consequences of the withdrawal of the recognition of a refugee status. According to the section, where the Board withdraws the refugee status of any person, the protection granted to him and his family shall cease fourteen days after he is notified of the withdrawal of status, or where an appeal has been made to the Secretary, the date on which he is notified of the Secretary's confirmation of the Board's decision. Any member of his family who may be affected by this withdrawal of status may themselves apply for refugee status.

205. Section 17 of PNDCL 305D provides other instances of the cessation of refugee status. It states that a person may also lose his refugee status if he voluntarily seeks the protection of or establishes himself in his country of origin, or acquires Ghanaian or other citizenship and enjoys the protection of his new nationality. If the circumstances under which his refugee status was granted cease to exist, he shall cease to be a refugee unless he can convince the Board that there are compelling reasons arising out of previous persecution for his failure to avail himself of the protection of his country of origin.

206. An asylum seeker who enters Ghana has to follow specific legal procedures and processes to obtain a refugee status. He must first declare his intention to seek refugee status at the point of entry into Ghana or if he did not enter the country through an approved point of entry, present himself to the nearest Immigration or UNHCR office within fourteen days. The UNHCR will provide interpreters for asylum seekers who cannot communicate in English. The asylum seeker has to fill out an IRF upon which he is given an appointment for the determination of his refugee status. His application is forwarded to the GRB which must notify the applicant in writing of its decision to grant or deny the application. The GRB may invite the applicant for an interview, at which time he is required to bring any identification that he may have. The applicant, upon receiving notice of the denial of his application, has thirty days to appeal this decision and may remain in Ghana with his family pending the decision from the GRB.

§3. Legal Position

207. PNDCL 305D provides a right of residence for refugees. Section 10 of that law states that 'notwithstanding the provisions of any other law, a person who has applied for recognition as a refugee, and every member of his family shall have the right to remain within Ghana until the person has been recognised as a refugee; or in the event of the application being unsuccessful, until the applicant has had the opportunity to exhaust his right of appeal under Section 9 or where an appeal has been dismissed, until the applicant has been allowed a reasonable time not exceeding three months, to seek admission to a country of his choice. The Secretary may on an application made to him by the person concerned, extend the three month period where he is satisfied that there is a reasonable likelihood of the person being admitted to a country of his choice within the extended period.'

208. Section 11(2) of PNDCL 305D further provides that a person who has been granted a refugee status under this Act and the members of the family shall, subject to the provisions of this Act be issued with identity cards in the prescribed form, a residence permit, United Nations Travel Document where appropriate, and be subject to all the laws in force in Ghana. Also, under PNDCL 305D and the international conventions on refugees that Ghana has ratified, a refugee, by reason of his or her refugee status, is accorded many rights and duties in Ghana. Section 1 of PNDCL 305D, protects refugees with regards to entry and expulsion measures. It provides that a refugee shall not be refused entry into or expelled from the Republic if that refusal of entry or expulsion places him in a country where his life or freedom is threatened on account of his race, religion, nationality, political or social affiliations or as result of external aggression, occupation or foreign domination in that country.

209. The exceptions are refugees who are dangerous to the security of the Republic, refugees who have committed serious non-political criminal offences outside the Republic and refugees who have been convicted of serious criminal offences in the Republic and pose a real danger to the public. Under section 3 of PNDCL 305D, a refugee may be detained or expelled for reasons of national security or public order, but a refugee shall not be expelled to a country where the refugee has reason to fear persecution. Also, if a refugee/asylum seeker enters Ghana through an unapproved route, he/she must proceed to the nearest immigration office for the necessary formalities after entry.

210. These rights and duties have been extensively set out in detail in the UN Convention Relating to the Status of Refugees 1951, the 1967 Protocol Relating to the Status of Refugees and the erstwhile OAU (now AU) Convention Governing the Specific Aspects of Refugee Problems in Africa. Section 11(1) of PNDCL 305D, adopts and makes these international laws applicable to refugees in Ghana. Furthermore, under the international conventions on refugees that Ghana has ratified, a refugee, by reason of his or her refugee status, is accorded many rights and duties in Ghana. These rights and duties have been extensively set out in detail in the UN Convention Relating to the Status of Refugees 1951, the 1967 Protocol Relating to the Status of Refugees and the erstwhile OAU (now AU) Convention Governing the Specific Aspects of Refugee Problems in Africa. Article 33 of the UN Convention Relating to the Status of Refugees 1951 provides that no Contracting State shall expel or return a refugee in any manner whatsoever to the frontiers of territories where his life or freedom would be threatened on account of his race, religion, nationality, membership of a particular social group or political opinion.

211. Article V of the OAU Convention makes provision for voluntary repatriation of refugees and stipulates that no refugee shall be repatriated against his will. Repatriation must necessarily be voluntary. When a refugee requests repatriation, the host country and country of origin shall make the necessary arrangements for his return. Upon his return, his country of origin shall facilitate his resettlement, giving him the full rights and privileges of nationals and shall under no circumstances penalize him for leaving. Indeed, he shall be assisted in every possible way by the host country and country of origin as well as by voluntary, international and intergovernmental agencies. An invitation to a normal and peaceful life without fear of disturbance or punishment shall be made to all refugees, when necessary, through the national information media and the Administrative Secretary-General of the O.A.U.

212. Article 30 of the UN Convention Relating to the Status of Refugees 1951 provides refugees the right to transfer their lawfully acquired assets to a country of their choice. It states that refugees shall be allowed to transfer their lawful assets from a Contracting State to the country of their resettlement, in conformity with the laws and regulations of each Contracting State. The Contracting States are to give sympathetic consideration to applications to transfer assets from their location to the country where the refugee has been admitted for resettlement.

213. Article 31 of the UN Convention focuses basically on the non-imposition of penalties on account of the illegal presence of refugees in a country and provides that refugees coming directly from a country in which their life or freedom is threatened shall not be penalized for illegal entry into a Contracting State as long as they promptly provide good cause to the authorities for their illegal entry. Their movements shall not be unnecessarily restricted during the period before their stay is regularized and they shall be allowed a reasonable time and opportunity to obtain admission to another country

214. Other relevant provisions of the UN Convention that address the subsidiary protection and humanitarian status of refugees include Articles 32 and 33 that provide that a lawful refugee cannot be expelled except pursuant to a national security or public order based decision reached in accordance with due process of law. The refugee shall be allowed to submit exculpatory evidence on his behalf to the designated authority over the proceedings. He shall also be allowed representation and the right to appeal to the designated authority. Further, he shall be allowed a reasonable time to obtain admission to another country, subject to whatever internal measures the Contracting State deems it necessary to place upon him. Under no circumstances shall he be returned to a country where his life or freedom is threatened on account of his race, religion, nationality, political or social affiliations. The benefit of this provision cannot be claimed by refugees who are dangerous to the security of the country or refugees who have been convicted of serious criminal offences in the country and pose a real danger to the public.

215. Articles 20–23 of the 1951 UN Convention deal with rights concerning the welfare of refugees in the receiving Contracting countries: According to the articles, where there is a rationing system for the distribution of products in short supply, refugees shall be accorded the same treatment as nationals.[112] In addition, lawful refugees shall be accorded the same treatment as nationals in the application of housing laws, or at the very least, the same treatment as aliens in the same circumstances. This shall be the case where housing laws are regulated by laws or regulations or are subject to the control of public authorities.[113]Furthermore, refugees shall be accorded the same treatment as nationals in matters of elementary education. With respect to education other than elementary education, specifically, as regards access to studies, the recognition of foreign school certificates, diplomas and degrees, the remission of fees and charges and the award of scholarships, they shall be accorded the same treatment as nationals, or at the very least, the same treatment as aliens.[114] It is important to note that Lawful refugees shall be accorded the same treatment as nationals in the application of public relief and assistance laws.[115]

216. Some of the relevant articles in these international laws with respect to a refugee's right to residence in Ghana include Article 11 of the 1951 UN Convention which provides for the right of refugee seamen: In the case of refugees regularly serving as crew members on board a ship flying the flag of a Contracting State, that State shall give sympathetic consideration to their establishment on its territory and the issue of travel documents to them or their temporary admission to its territory particularly with a view to facilitating their establishment in another country. Ghana's approach to residence permits for refugees and their freedom of movement, follow the rules in the 1951 UN Convention which Ghana is a signatory. Article 26 deals with Freedom of Movement and requires each Contracting State to accord refugees lawfully in its territory the right to choose their place of residence and to move freely within its territory, subject to regulations applicable to aliens generally in the same circumstances. Article 27 requires the Contracting States to issue identity papers to any refugee in their territory who does not possess a valid travel document. On the issue of Travel Documents, it is the duty of the Contracting States to issue to refugees lawfully staying in their territory travel documents for the purpose of travel outside their territory unless compelling reasons of national security or public order otherwise require. The Contracting States may issue such a travel document to any other refugee in their territory they shall in particular give sympathetic consideration to the issue of such a travel document to refugees in their territory who are unable to obtain a travel document from the country of their lawful residence. Travel documents issued to refugees under previous international agreements by parties thereto shall be recognized and treated by the Contracting States in the same way as if they had been issued pursuant to this article.

---

112. *See* Art. 20 of the UN Convention Relating to the Status of Refugees 1951.
113. *See* Art. 21 of the UN Convention Relating to the Status of Refugees 1951.
114. *See* Art. 22 of the UN Convention Relating to the Status of Refugees 1951.
115. *See* Art. 23 of the UN Convention Relating to the Status of Refugees 1951.

217. Article 2 of the 1951 UN Convention provides that, every refugee has duties to the country in which he finds himself, which require in particular that he conforms to its laws and regulations as well as to measures taken for the maintenance of public order. Also, Article 111 of the OAU (now AU) Convention stipulates that every refugee has duties to the country in which he finds himself which require in particular that he conforms to its laws and regulations as well as measures taken for the maintenance of public order including abstaining from any subversive activities against any Member State of the AU. Thus, refugees residing in AU states are prohibited from attacking any State Member by any activity likely to cause tension between Member States, and in particular by use of arms, or through the mass media.

218. In Ghana, the general duties of a citizen as laid down in Article 41 of the 1992 Constitution applies to a person granted refugee status as well, and these duties include:

(a) to promote the prestige and good name of Ghana and respect the symbols of the nation;
(b) to uphold and defend this Constitution and the law;
(c) to foster national unity and live in harmony with others;
(d) to respect the rights, freedoms and legitimate interest of others and generally to refrain from doing acts detrimental to the welfare of other persons;
(e) to work conscientiously in his or her lawfully chosen occupation;
(f) to protect and preserve public property and expose and combat misuse and waste of public funds and property;
(g) to contribute to the well-being of the community where the citizen lives;
(h) to defend Ghana and render national service when necessary; to co-operate with lawful agencies in the maintenance of law and order; to declare his or her income honestly to the appropriate and lawful agencies and to satisfy all tax obligations; and to protect and safeguard the environment.

219. An integral part of the right to residence is the right not to be discriminated against on the grounds of race, religion, etc. Both the UN and OAU Conventions have provisions on non-discrimination. Articles 3 and IV of the UN and OAU Conventions respectively provide that the Contracting States shall apply the provisions of the Convention to refugees without discrimination as to race, religion or country of origin, membership of a particular social group or political opinions. Moreover, Chapter five of the 1992 Constitution of Ghana, which is headed protection of fundamental human rights and freedoms, buttress this principle of non-discrimination and provides in Article 17 that all persons shall be equal before the law. A person shall not be discriminated against on grounds of gender, race, colour, ethnic origin, religion, creed or social or economic status. For the purposes of Article 17, 'discriminate' means to give different treatment to different persons attributable only or mainly to their respective descriptions by race, place of origin, political opinions, colour, gender, occupation, religion or creed, whereby persons of one description are subjected to disabilities or restrictions to which persons of another description are not made subject or are granted privileges or advantages which are not granted to persons of another description.

220. The right not to be discriminated against on religious grounds is further strengthened by Article 4 of the UN Convention on the right of freedom of religion. It provides that the Contracting States shall accord to refugees within their territories treatment at least as favourable as that accorded to their nationals with respect to freedom to practice their religion and freedom as regards the religious education of their children. The standard applicable here is the national treatment standard, as states are to provide treatment at least as favourable as that accorded to their nationals. Therefore if a country strictly practices one religion to the exclusion of all others, then that country would not be required to make special provision for refugees as that is the standard accorded to its nationals and the requirement is that at least the treatment must be at par with that accorded nationals. Ghana is a country where the freedom to practice one's choice of religion is granted and provided for in Article 21(c) of the 1992 Constitution to the effect that all persons in Ghana shall have the right to freedom to practice any religion and to manifest such practice.

221. Article 5 of the UN Convention provides that nothing in this Convention shall be deemed to impair any rights and benefits granted by a Contracting State to refugees apart from this Convention. Therefore where a contracting State has other regulations that add up to the rights of refugees, though not specifically provided for by the Convention, refugees shall still be entitled to such rights. The Convention is therefore the basic and should not be derogated from, however, it can be added to. Moreover, Article 7 is on the right to be exempted from reciprocity. So, except where the Convention contains more favourable provisions, a Contracting State shall accord to refugees the same treatment as is accorded to aliens generally. And after a period of three years' residence, all refugees shall enjoy exemption from legislative reciprocity in the territory of the Contracting States. Each Contracting State shall continue to accord to refugees the rights and benefits to which they were already entitled, in the absence of reciprocity, at the date of entry into force of this Convention for that State. The Contracting States shall consider favourably the possibility of according to refugees, in the absence of reciprocity, rights and benefits beyond those to which they are entitled in Article 7, and to extending exemption from reciprocity to refugees who do not fulfil the conditions provided for in Article 7.

222. Article 8 is on the refugees' right to be exempted from exceptional measures which may be taken against the person, property or interests of nationals of a foreign State. The Contracting States shall not apply such measures to a refugee who is formally a national of the said foreign State solely on account of such nationality. Contracting States which, under their legislation, are prevented from applying the general principle expressed in this Article, shall, in appropriate cases, grant exemptions in favour of such refugees. Articles 12–19 of the 1951 UN Convention are on the *judicial status* of a refugee.

Personal Status

223. The personal status of a refugee is governed by the laws of the country of his domicile first, and then by the laws of the country of his residence. His previously acquired personal rights, especially those regarding marriage, shall be respected by Contracting States, subject to compliance with the formalities required by the laws of his domicile or country of residence, and if those rights would have been recognized by the laws of his domicile or country of residence had he not become a refugee.[116]

Movable and Immovable Property and Intellectual Property Rights

224. Refugees shall be treated at least as favourably as aliens, regarding the acquisition of real and personal property, related contracts and their attendant rights.[117]With respect to intellectual property rights, in his host country, a refugee shall be accorded the same treatment as nationals of his host country. In any other Contracting State, he shall be accorded the same treatment as nationals of his host country.[118]

Rights of Association and Access to Courts

225. Contracting States shall accord lawful refugees the most favourable treatment accorded to nationals of a foreign country in matters relating to non-political and non-profit-making associations and trade unions.[119] In addition, Contracting States shall accord refugees the same treatment as nationals regarding access to the courts of law, including legal assistance and exemption from *cautio judicatum solvi*, i.e., payment of security for legal costs or other litigation security measures. In any other Contracting State, he shall be accorded the same treatment as the nationals of the country of his habitual residence.[120]

Gainful/Self-employment

226. Contracting States shall accord lawful refugees the most favourable treatment accorded to nationals of a foreign country in matters relating to the right to engage in wage-earning employment. Restrictions to protect the national labour market shall not be imposed on any refugee who has been in the host country for three years or who is married to a national of the host country or who has one or more children that are nationals of the host country. Nor shall restrictions be imposed on any refugee who was already exempt from them at the date of entry into force of this Convention for the Contracting State. The Contracting States shall give sympathetic consideration to the assimilation of the rights of all refugees relating to

---

116. *See* Art. 12 of the UN Convention Relating to the Status of Refugees 1951.
117. *See* Art. 13 of the UN Convention Relating to the Status of Refugees 1951.
118. *See* Art. 14 of the UN Convention Relating to the Status of Refugees 1951.
119. *See* Art. 15 of the UN Convention Relating to the Status of Refugees 1951.
120. *See* Art. 16 of the UN Convention Relating to the Status of Refugees 1951.

wage-earning employment into those of nationals, especially those who have entered the Contracting State pursuant to labour recruitment programmes or immigration schemes.[121] Also, Contracting States shall accord lawful refugees the most favourable treatment accorded to nationals of a foreign country in matters relating to the right to self-employ in agriculture, industry, handicrafts and commerce and to establish commercial and industrial ventures.[122]

Liberal Professions

227. Contracting States shall accord lawful refugees who hold diplomas recognized by the competent authorities of that State, and who are desirous of practising a liberal profession, treatment as favourable as possible, but no less favourable than that accorded to aliens generally. [123]

Labour Legislation and Social Security

228. Contracting States shall accord refugees national treatment in matters relating to remuneration, including family allowances; overtime arrangements, paid holidays, restrictions on home-work, minimum age of employment, apprenticeship and training, women's work and collective bargaining agreements, insofar as such matters are governed by laws or regulations. Refugees shall also be accorded national treatment regarding social security matters (legal provisions in respect of employment injury, occupational diseases, maternity, sickness, disability, old age, death, unemployment, family responsibilities and any other contingency which according to national laws or regulations, is covered by a social security scheme) taking into account arrangements for the maintenance of acquired rights and rights in course of acquisition, and special arrangements concerning benefits payable wholly out of public funds, and allowances paid to persons who do not fulfil the contribution conditions prescribed for the award of a normal pension. The right to receive compensation for the death of a refugee due to employment injury or occupational disease shall not be affected by the beneficiary's residence outside the Contracting State. Contracting States shall also accord to refugees the benefits of present and future agreements regarding acquired rights and rights in the process of acquisition dealing with social security subject only to the conditions which apply to nationals of the States signatory to the agreements in question. Further, they shall give sympathetic consideration to according refugees the benefits of similar agreements in force between such Contracting States and non-contracting States.[124]

229. According to Article 25, when a refugee, during the exercise of a right, cannot have recourse to the assistance of the authorities of a foreign country which he would normally require, the Contracting State where he resides shall arrange for its own authorities or an international authority to provide the refugee with the neces

121. *See* Art. 17 of the UN Convention Relating to the Status of Refugees 1951.
122. *See* Art. 18 of the UN Convention Relating to the Status of Refugees 1951.
123. *See* Art. 19 of the UN Convention Relating to the Status of Refugees 1951.
124. *See* Art. 24 of the UN Convention Relating to the Status of Refugees 1951.

sary assistance. The Contracting State shall cause the delivery of documentation or certifications to the refugee as would normally be delivered to aliens by their national authorities. Such documentation or certification shall serve in place of the official instruments delivered to aliens by their national authorities and shall be valid for the purpose absent evidence to the contrary. Moderate fees shall be charged for these services, commensurate with the fees charged to nationals for similar services. Indigent persons shall be granted necessary exceptions.

230. According to Article 29 of the UN Convention, the Contracting States are not permitted to impose upon refugee‘s duties, charges or taxes, of any description whatsoever, other or higher than those which are or may be levied on their nationals in similar situations. But this injunction on fiscal charges shall not prevent the application to refugees of the laws and regulations concerning charges in respect of the issue to aliens of administrative documents including identity papers. Also, Article 34 of the UN Convention provides that the Contracting States shall as far as possible facilitate the assimilation and naturalization of refugees, and they shall in particular make every effort to expedite naturalization proceedings and to reduce as far as possible the charges and costs of such proceedings.

§4. Position of Family Members

231. PNDCL 305D makes provision for the family members of refugees in Ghana to join them. Section 26, which is the interpretation section of PNDCL 305D, defines a family member in relation to a refugee to mean the following: ‘any spouse of the refugee; any unmarried child of the refugee under the age of 18 years; or any other person who is related to the refugee by blood or marriage and who by reason of old age, infirmity or minority is dependent upon the refugee.’ According to section 10 of PNDCL 305D, notwithstanding the provisions of any other law, a person who has applied for recognition as a refugee, and every member of his family shall have the right to remain within Ghana until the person has been recognized as a refugee; or in the event of the application being unsuccessful, until the applicant has had the opportunity to exhaust his right of appeal; or where an appeal has been dismissed, until the applicant has been allowed a reasonable time not exceeding three months, to seek admission to a country of his choice, and the period of application may be extended where the Secretary is satisfied that there is a reasonable likelihood of the person being admitted to a country of his choice within the extended period. Section 11(2)of PNDCL 305D further provides that ‘a person who has been granted a refugee status under this Act and the members of the family shall, subject to the provisions of this Act be (a) issued with identity cards in the prescribed form, (b) issued with a residence permit, (c) issued with the United Nations Travel Document where appropriate, and (d) subject to all the laws in force in Ghana’. Section 12 also has provisions relating to family members of recognized refugees:

(1) A member of the family of a person granted refugee status in Ghana shall subject to the provisions of this Law be permitted to remain in Ghana for as long as the refugee is permitted to remain in Ghana and shall be entitled to the same benefits and right as the refugee.
(2) Where a member of the family of the refugee is within Ghana by virtue of subsection (1) and the member ceases to be a family member by reason of marriage, attainment of age of majority or the cessation of the dependence on the refugee, the member shall be permitted to continue to remain in Ghana.
(3) On the death of the person with refugee status or on that person's divorce or legal separation from a spouse, a person who immediately before the death, divorce or legal separation was within Ghana by virtue of this section as a member of the family of the refugee shall be permitted to continue to remain in Ghana.
(4) A person who has been permitted to remain in Ghana by virtue of subsections (2) and (3) may apply for a refugee status.

232. Section 13 of PNDCL 305D further provides that the Minister may, by notice in the Gazette or by any other means appropriate, designate places and areas in Ghana where (a) persons with refugee status, (b) persons who have applied under the Act for refugee status, and (c) *members of the families* of persons referred to in (a) and (b) above, or any class of refugees shall live. Moreover, where the GRB has by virtue of section 15 withdrawn the recognition of a person as a refugee, then, based on section 16(1) of that law, that person shall cease to be a refugee, and the protection granted to members of that person's family, shall cease with effect from (a) fourteen days after the date on which the Board notified the person concerned of the withdrawal of recognition, or (b) where an appeal has been lodged with the Minister under sub-section (3) of section 15, the date on which the Minister notifies the refugee confirming the decision of the Board. Be that as it may, section 16(2) provides that a member of the family who may be affected by section 16 may apply for refugee status.

Part IV. Loss of Right of Residence

Chapter 1. Conditions under Which the Right of Residence Might Be Lost

233. Section 13(2) of the *Immigration Act, 2000 (Act 573*) provides that the Director may grant a residence permit for up to a period not exceeding eight years, except that a residence permit shall not be for more than four years in the first instance. Thus ordinary residence is time-bound and may be lost unless renewed. Section 20(1) of the Act therefore provides that a person shall not remain in Ghana after the expiration of a permit issued to that person. The expiration of a permit may therefore result in a loss of residence in Ghana. Section 23 of *Act 573* provides for the renewal of permits and stipulates that a person who has been granted a permit to remain in Ghana under this Act may, within one month before the permit expires, apply to the Director in the prescribed manner for a renewal of the permit (section 23(1) *of Act 573*). An application for a renewal of a permit shall be treated as an application for a permit under section 4(1) of *Act 573*, but the Director may renew the permit with effect from the date of issue or from the date of expiry of the previous permit (section 23(2)).

234. Section 20(2) provides that subject to section 19 of *Act 573*, the Director may, during the period of validity of a permit or visa granted to a person permitting that person to enter or remain in Ghana, (a) revoke the permit on grounds of fraudulent misrepresentation or concealment or any other illegal practice, (b) revoke the permit on grounds that the conditions governing the permit have been breached, or (c) impose new conditions in relation to that permit, and shall take reasonable steps to communicate the notice of revocation, or the new conditions, to the person concerned. Thus, if the new conditions are not complied with by the permit holder, the permit may be revoked under the authority of section 19(1)(b) of *Act 573* on the grounds that the conditions governing the issuing of the permit have been breached.

235. A person who has been granted a right of abode in Ghana may lose that status as provided for in section 19 of *Act 573*. Section 19 of that Act provides that the High Court may, on application by the Attorney-General, deprive a person of a right of abode status on the grounds that (a) the activities of that person are inimical to the security of the State or prejudicial to public order, public health, morality or public interest, or (b) the right was acquired by fraudulent misrepresentation or any other illegal or irregular means, or (c) the holder of the status no longer qualifies under the Act.

236 Part I, Ch. 1, Conditions under Which the Right of Residence Might Be Lost

236. Section 15(3) of *Act 573*, provides that a person who is granted an indefinite residence status leaves Ghana for more than twelve consecutive months loses that status automatically. Section 16(3) of Act 573 provides that where a foreign spouse who has been granted an indefinite residence status has left Ghana for more than twelve consecutive months, that foreigner spouse automatically loses that status. However, the separation, divorce or death of a spouse in a marriage to which section 16s indefinite residence status for foreign spouses does not affect the indefinite residence status held by the foreign spouse immediately before the occurrence of the event.

Chapter 2. Legal and Administrative Procedures

237. The *Immigration Act, 2000 (Act 573)* and the *Immigration Regulations, 2001 (L.I. 1691)* provide detailed rules on the administrative procedures that may lead to the loss of the right of residence. Residence may be lost automatically if the passing of time results in the expiration of a permit. A person whose permit expires is not allowed to remain in Ghana as stipulated in section 20(1) of *Act 573*, unless the permit is renewed. Under sections 15(3) and 16(3) of *Act 573* a person granted an indefinite residence status or a foreign spouse who has been granted an indefinite residence status may respectively lose his or her residence automatically, if he or she leaves Ghana for more than twelve consecutive months.

238. As discussed in paragraph 234 of Part IV, the Director may, during the period of validity of a permit or visa granted to a person permitting that person to enter or remain in Ghana, revoke the permit on grounds of fraudulent misrepresentation or concealment or any other illegal practice, or on the grounds that the conditions governing the permit have been breached (section 20(2) of Act 573). However, any such revocation must follow the procedure as stipulated in section 19 of Act 573 where the High Court may, on application by the Attorney-General, deprive a person of their right of abode, indefinite residence or residence status on the grounds that (a) the activities of that person are inimical to the security of the State or prejudicial to public order, public health, morality or public interest, (b) the right was acquired by fraudulent misrepresentation or any other illegal or irregular means, or (c) the holder of the status no longer qualifies under the Act.

239. Section 20(2) of *Act 573* requires the Director to take reasonable steps to communicate the notice of revocation to the person concerned. Section 20(3) of Act 573 then provides that where a permit is revoked and notice has been given and the holder of that permit is (a) present in Ghana, the holder shall not remain in Ghana after the revocation and shall be removed from Ghana in accordance with the provisions of this and be prohibited from re-entering Ghana temporarily, or in the case of a prohibited immigrant, permanently; or (b) where the holder of that permit is outside Ghana, the holder shall be prohibited from re-entering Ghana temporarily, or in the case of a prohibited immigrant, permanently. A person who enters or re-enters or remains in Ghana in contravention of a revocation and/or removal order made under section 20 of *Act 573*, commits an offence and is liable on summary conviction to pay a fine of no less than fifty penalty units or to a term of imprisonment of not less than three months or more than one year. Where a permit is revoked the revocation applies to (a) the person whose name is endorsed in the permit, (b) the spouse of the holder of the permit where the spouse was issued a permit as consequence of the issuing of a permit to the other spouse, and (c) the dependant of the holder of the permit who is not a citizen (section 20(5) of *Act 573*). Section 20(6) of *Act 573* states that notification of a revocation order to the holder of the permit constitutes notification to the persons mentioned in sub-section (5).

Section 35 of *Act 573* provides rules on the persons liable to deportation. Under section 35(1) of *Act 573*, a foreign national is liable to deportation if (a) a court recommendation for his deportation is effective under sub-section (2) of this section;

(b) he has been found by a court to be destitute or without means of support or to be of unsound mind or mentally handicapped; (c) he is a prohibited immigrant; (d) he is in Ghana without a valid permit, or any of the conditions subject to which his permit was granted has been broken; or (e) his presence in Ghana is, in the opinion of the Minister, not conducive to the public good. Where a court makes a finding under paragraph (b) of sub-section (1) (that the foreign national is destitute or without means of support or of unsound mind or mentally handicapped), that court must report the finding in writing to the Minister (section 35(3) of *Act 573*).

240. Section 35(2) of *Act 573* provides that a recommendation for deportation is effective if it is made by a court upon conviction for an offence punishable by a term of imprisonment exceeding three months with or without a fine and (a) on an appeal against the conviction, the appellate court has upheld the recommendation; or (b) no appeal has been brought within the time allowed for appeal, but the recommendation was made by (i) the High Court, or (ii) inferior lower court and has been approved by the Chief Justice. Sections 36 and 37 of *Act 573* provide detailed rules on how a deportation order may be made and the effect of such an order.

Deportation Order

241. The Minister may, by executive instrument, order the deportation of any person liable to deportation, including his dependants, subject to such conditions as the Minister may impose.[125]

Effect of Deportation Order

242. The deportee has to leave Ghana and is not allowed to return as long as the deportation order remains in force. Returning to Ghana during the period when this is not permitted according to the deportation order is a criminal offence punishable by a five-year maximum prison sentence and re-deportation under the original deportation order. Unless the Minister directs otherwise, a deportee who is serving a prison sentence shall complete the sentence before being deported.[126]

Supervision Order

243. If a deportation is not carried out within six months after it was ordered, or if, during that period, the Minister considers that deportation is impracticable, or undesirable, he may, by executive instrument, make a supervision order requiring the deportee to observe the conditions regarding his place of residence, his political activities, periodic reporting to immigration officials and police, his means of employment and his association with criminals. If the deportee is serving a prison sentence, the six month period starts at the end of his term of imprisonment. Failing to comply with the terms of a supervision order is a criminal offence punishable by a two month maximum prison sentence, a fine or both. A supervision order sus

125. *See* s. 36 of the Immigration Act, 2000 (Act 573).
126. *See* s. 37 of the Immigration Act, 2000 (Act 573).

pends a deportation order until the Minister revives the deportation order., In all cases a supervision order expires after a period of two years, upon which the underlying deportation order also expires.[127]

127. *See* s. 40 of the Immigration Act, 2000 (Act 573).

Part V. Sanctions

Chapter 1. Sanctions

§1. Administrative Sanctions

244. According to section 8(4)(a) of *Act 573,* an immigration officer may prevent a prohibited immigrant from entering Ghana, or if the prohibited immigrant has already entered Ghana, direct the prohibited immigrant to depart from Ghana using the first available means. Any force that is necessary to ensure compliance with the directions of the immigration officer may be used. Where an immigration officer directs a prohibited immigrant to depart from Ghana using the first available means under section 8(4)(a), that officer may, at the same time, direct the person in charge or the owner or agent of any vessel, vehicle or aircraft from which the prohibited immigrant disembarked to remove that immigrant from Ghana using the first available means (section 8(5) of *Act 573*).

245. Undersection 8(4)(c) of *Act 573*, an immigration officer can arrest a prohibited immigrant without a warrant and effectuate the repatriation or bring the prohibited immigrant before a Court for an offence under section 8(2) of *Act 573*. Section 21 of *Act 573*, which is entitled '*The Removal of Illegal Immigrants*,' also provides that, where the presence of a person in Ghana is unlawful, that person may be repatriated from Ghana by an order of the Director. Under section 36(1) of *Act 573*, the Minister may, by executive instrument, order the deportation of a person liable to deportation. Section 35(1) of *Act 573* provides that a foreign national is liable to deportation if he is in Ghana without a valid permit, or where any of the conditions subject to which his permit was granted has been breached; or his presence in Ghana is, in the opinion of the Minister, not conducive to the public good or a court recommendation for his deportation has been given. A deportation order may include the dependants of the person to be deported if the Minister so directs.

246. According to section 20(3)(a) of the *Immigration Act, 2000 (Act 573*), where a permit is revoked and notice is given and the holder of that permit is present in Ghana, the holder is not entitled to remain in Ghana after the revocation order has been issued. That person is removed from Ghana in accordance with the provisions of *Act 573* and is prohibited from re-entering Ghana temporarily, or, in the case of a prohibited immigrant, permanently. However, if the holder of the revoked permit is outside Ghana, the holder is prohibited from re-entering Ghana temporarily, or, in the case of a prohibited immigrant, permanently. Under section 20(5) of *Act 573*, where a permit is revoked, the revocation order applies to any person whose name is endorsed in the permit, a spouse of the holder of the permit where the spouse was issued a permit as a consequence of the issuing of a permit to the other spouse, and a dependant of the holder of the permit who is not a citizen of Ghana. Moreover, according to section 20(6) of *Act 573*, notification of a revocation order to the holder of the permit constitutes the notification of that order to the aforementioned persons.

247. Undersection 15(3) of *Act 573*, where a person is granted an indefinite residence status and he leaves Ghana for more than twelve consecutive months he loses that status automatically. Section 16(3) of Act 573 provides that where a foreign spouse who is granted an indefinite residence status has left Ghana for more than twelve consecutive months, that foreigner spouse automatically loses that status. However, if the reason for leaving Ghana is due to continuous education or medical care abroad or any other satisfactory ground, then, upon application to the Director, the loss of the residence status may be reviewed and restored.

248. Section 49 of *Act 573* provides that the Minister may, by legislative instrument, declare some areas in Ghana as prohibited to foreign nationals. In such cases, a foreign national may not enter or remain in those areas designated as prohibited to foreigners unless he has a valid prohibited area permit granted by the appropriate authority. Such a permit shall be subject to any condition as specified in the permit, and shall be issued in a prescribed form.

§2. Penal Sanctions

249. Section 3(5) of the *Immigration Act, 2000, Act 573*, states that without prejudice to any other penalty imposed by or under this Act, a person who enters Ghana through an unapproved route commits an offence and is liable on summary conviction to a fine of no less than fifty penalty units, a term of imprisonment of no less than three months and not exceeding twelve months or to both, the fine and the term of imprisonment. Section 7(3) of *Act 573* provides a person who refuses or neglects to comply with a direction given by an immigration officer, or who leaves the detention area in contravention of section 7(1) of *Act 573*, commits an offence and may be penalized on summary conviction to a fine not exceeding 250 penalty units or to a term of imprisonment for a term not exceeding twelve months or both to the fine and the term of imprisonment. Under section 7(1) of *Act 573*, an immigration officer, if in doubt as to the right of a person to enter Ghana, may order that person to be detained, and to remain in custody pending the determination of the matter.

250. Section 8(2) of Act 573 provides that a person who enters Ghana as a prohibited immigrant commits an offence and is liable, on summary conviction, to a fine not exceeding 500 penalty units, to a term of imprisonment of no less than six months and not exceeding two years or to both the fine and the term of imprisonment. Under section 8(5) of *Act 573*, an immigration officer may order a prohibited immigrant to leave Ghana using the first available means, and may, at the same time, order the person in charge or the owner or agent of any vessel, vehicle or aircraft from which the prohibited immigrant disembarked to remove that immigrant from Ghana using the first available means. If such a person fails to comply with the order to remove the prohibited immigrant from Ghana using the first available means, he will commit an offence and may be liable, on summary conviction, to a fine not exceeding 250 penalty units, to a term of imprisonment not exceeding twelve months or to both the fine and the term of imprisonment under section 8(6) of *Act 573*.

251. When a permit to reside in Ghana has expired or has been revoked, the holder of such a permit who enters, re-enters or remains in Ghana commits an offence and is liable, on summary conviction, to a fine of no less than fifty penalty units or to a term of imprisonment of not less than three months or more than one year (section 20(4) of *Act 573*). Under section 37(2) of *Act 573*, a person who enters Ghana when a deportation order made against him is in force commits an offence and is liable, on summary conviction, to a term of imprisonment not exceeding five years and may be deported without any further deportation order being made. Section 49 of *Act 573* prohibits a foreign national from entering or remaining in areas prohibited to foreigners unless he has a valid prohibited area permit granted by the appropriate authority. A person who contravenes section 49 of *Act 573* commits an offence and is, on summary conviction, liable to a term of imprisonment of no less than three months, to a fine of no less than twenty-five penalty units or to both the term of imprisonment and the fine.

252. Regulation 18 of the *Immigration Regulations 2001(L.I. 1691*) provides various fines as a penalty for illegal employment of foreigners in Ghana where not permitted by *Act 573*. Under section 52A of the *Immigration (Amendment) Act, 2012 (Act 848*) migrant smuggling is prohibited and a person who engages in migrant smuggling commits an offence and is liable on conviction to a fine of not less than 620 penalty units and not more than 1,250 penalty units, to a term of imprisonment of no less than five years and no more than ten years or to both. Section 52 of *Act 573* lists a number of actions that may constitute an offence under *Act 573* and prescribes a fine or imprisonment of no more than two years or both for any such offence.

§3. Detention

253. Undersection 7(1) of *Act 573*, where an immigration officer is in doubt as to the right of a person to enter Ghana, the officer may send that person to be detained, and that person remains in custody pending the determination of the matter. A person who refuses or neglects to comply with a direction given by an immigration officer under that section, or who leaves the detention area in contravention of that section, commits an offence and may be penalized, on summary conviction, to a fine not exceeding 250 penalty units, to a term of imprisonment for a term not exceeding twelve months or to both the fine and the term of imprisonment (section

7(3) of *Act 573*). However, under section 7(2) of that Act, the Director may, pending the completion of enquiries in respect of a detained person, release that person from custody under the conditions as determined by the Director and may, for that purpose, issue a temporary permit to that person.

254. An immigration officer is further empowered to direct a prohibited immigrant not to disembark from any ship, vehicle or aircraft on which the prohibited immigrant may be, or not to depart from any place, except to go to some other place approved of by the immigration officer (section 8(4)(b) of *Act 573*). According to section 8(7) of the Act, the person to whom any such instruction is given is deemed to be in lawful custody. Section 43 of *Act 573* then provides that where a person is in immigration custody under that Act, the master, owner, charterer and agent of the vessel or aircraft which brought that person to Ghana are jointly and severally liable for all expenses incurred due to the detention and maintenance of that person, unless the person detained is subsequently permitted to enter Ghana., section 43(2) of *Act 573* makes any such expenses recoverable as a debt due to the government by the master, owner, charterer and agent of the vessel or aircraft jointly and severally.

255. Section 21(2) and (3) of the *Immigration Act* provide that where the removal of a person from Ghana has been ordered due to his unlawful presence, that person may be arrested and detained for a period that is necessary to make arrangements for the removal. In such a case a person may be detained at a police station or in an immigration detention area. Section 22 of *Act 573* provides that an immigration officer enforcing the *Immigration Act* has the authority and powers of a police officer relating to arrest, detention and search. As has been discussed under the *Penal Sanctions supra*, penal measures for unlawful entry into Ghana may include a term of imprisonment under *Act 573*.

256. In section 8(2) of *Act 573*, a person who enters Ghana as a prohibited immigrant commits an offence and is liable, on summary conviction, to a fine not exceeding 500 penalty units, to a term of imprisonment of no less than six months and not exceeding two years, or to both the fine and the term of imprisonment. Under section 8(6) of *Act 573*, if the person in charge or the owner or agent of any vessel, vehicle or aircraft from which a prohibited immigrant disembarked, fails to remove that immigrant from Ghana using the first available means, as directed by an immigration officer, commits an offence and may be liable, on summary conviction, to a fine not exceeding 250 penalty units, to a term of imprisonment not exceeding twelve months, or to both the fine and the term of imprisonment. According to section 37(2) of *Act 573*, a person who enters Ghana when a deportation order that has been made against him is in force commits an offence and is liable, on summary conviction, to a term of imprisonment not exceeding five years and may be deported without any further deportation order being made.

§4. Expulsion and Removal

257. According to section 8(4)(a) of *Act 573*, an immigration officer may prevent a prohibited immigrant from entering Ghana, or, if the prohibited immigrant has already entered Ghana, order the prohibited immigrant to depart from Ghana by the first available means, and may use all necessary force to ensure compliance with the directive. Where an immigration officer orders a prohibited immigrant to leave Ghana by the first available means, that officer may, at the same time, order the person in charge or the owner or agent of any vessel, vehicle or aircraft from which the prohibited immigrant disembarked *to remove that immigrant from Ghana by the first available means* (section 8(5) of *Act 573*). Under section 8(4)(c) of *Act 573*, an immigration officer *may arrest a prohibited immigrant without a warrant and effect the repatriation* or bring the prohibited immigrant before a Court for an offence under section 8(2) of *Act 573*.

258. According to section 21(1) of *Act 573,* where the presence of a person in Ghana is unlawful, that person may be repatriated from Ghana by an order of the Director. Under section 36(1) of *Act 573* the Minister may, by executive instrument, order the deportation of any person liable to deportation (*see* paragraphs 265–269 and 367–368 *infra*). According to section 37(2) of *Act 573*a person who enters Ghana when a deportation order that has been made against him is in force commits an offence and is liable, on summary conviction, to a term of imprisonment not exceeding five years and may be deported without any further deportation order being made.

Removal of Illegal Immigrants

259. Where a person is in Ghana unlawfully, he may be repatriated by an order from the Director and may be arrested or detained in a police station or immigration detention facility while the arrangements for his repatriation are being made.[128]For this purpose an immigration office has the necessary authority to arrest, detain and search.[129]

Power to Arrest

260. Persons under supervision orders are not liable to arrest and detention. While in custody, the person to be deported may be conducted to or from any consulate or other place if this is necessary to determine his nationality or to facilitate his admission into another country. The deportee may be placed on a vessel or aircraft and detained there while in Ghana's territorial limits.[130] When a person who is to be deported is in custody, he may be photographed, measured and fingerprinted to ascertain his identity.[131]

---

128. Section 21 of the Immigration Act, 2000 (Act 573).
129. Section 22 of the Immigration Act, 2000 (Act 573).
130. Section 38 of the Immigration Act, 2000 (Act 573).
131. Section 39 of the Immigration Act, 2000 (Act 573).

Expenses of Deportation

261. The Director may use the deportee's money or property to pay the deportation expenses.

The person in charge, the owner and the agent of a vessel, aircraft or vehicle who brings a person to Ghana shall be jointly and severally liable for the deportation expenses of that person if the person was a crew member of that vessel or aircraft and was left in Ghana contrary to section 42 of *Act 573*, or if the person has already been deported or ordered to leave Ghana under section 8(4) of this Act. Any other person who is involved with bringing a prohibited immigrant into Ghana shall be liable for the person's deportation expenses.[132]

Section 3 of *PNDCL 305D (Refugees Law)* explains that a refugee can be detained or expelled for reasons of national security or public order, but should, under no circumstances, be expelled to a country where he has reason to fear persecution.

262. Section 40(4) and (5) of *Act 573* provides that the operation of a deportation order made in respect of any person shall be suspended while a supervision order is in force in relation to that person, but shall revive if the Minister so directs. In that case the supervision order shall cease to have effect. Moreover, subject to the aforementioned section 40(4), a supervision order made in respect of any person expires after a period of two years from the date of the issuing of that order. On the expiration of the supervision order, the deportation order made in respect of that person also expires.

263. According to section 21(1) of *Act 573,* where the presence of a person in Ghana is unlawful, that person may be repatriated from Ghana by an order of the Director. However, the *Human Trafficking Act, 2005 (Act 694)* makes an exception to the 'removal of an illegal immigrant' provisions in section 21 of the Immigration Act, 2000 (*Act 573*). Section 34(1) of the *Human Trafficking Act, 2005 (Act 694)*, provides that, notwithstanding the provisions in section 21 of the *Immigration Act, 2000 (Act 573*), a trafficked person who is in Ghana unlawfully, may remain in Ghana throughout the period of a legal investigation and prosecution of a trafficker. The Management Board shall make arrangements for the repatriation of the trafficked person upon completion of the legal process. A trafficked person may be repatriated to his or her country of origin upon the conviction of a trafficker. Until the repatriation can be effectuated, the trafficked persons remain in a reception centre provided by the Ministry of Interior where basic material support is provided (section 34(3) of the *Human Trafficking Act, 2005 (Act 694)*). Under section 3 of the *Refugees Law, 1992* (*PNDCL 305D*), a refugee may be detained or expelled for reasons of national security or public order. Under no circumstances shall a refugee be expelled to a country where he has reason to fear persecution.

264. Under section 36(1) of *Act 573*, the Minister may, by executive instrument, order the deportation of any person liable to deportation. A deportation order may

132. Section 41 of the Immigration Act, 2000 (Act 573).

include the dependants of the person to be deported if the Minister so directs under section 36(3) of *Act 573*. A person to be deported must leave Ghana in accordance with the requirements of the deportation order and must, as long as the deportation order is in force, remain outside Ghana (section 37(1) of the Act). According to section 37(2) of *Act 573*a person who enters Ghana when a deportation order made against him is in force commits an offence and is liable on summary conviction to a term of imprisonment not exceeding five years. That person may be deported without any further deportation order being made against him.

Person Liable to Deportation

265. The provisions on deportation in *Act 573* provide that a foreign national is liable to deportation if a court of law finds the foreign national guilty of an offence that is punishable by a term of imprisonment exceeding three months. Though the foreigner has a right to appeal his conviction, the recommendation for deportation made by the court is effective if the appellate court upholds it. The recommendation, if made by the High Court or a Lower Court, with the approval of the Chief Justice, is equally effective if the foreign national fails to appeal his conviction within the time allowed for an appeal. A foreign national is liable to deportation if he is found by a court to be either destitute, mentally handicapped or a prohibited immigrant. Additionally, a foreigner may be deported if he is in Ghana without a valid permit or if the authorized Minister of State determines that his presence in the country is 'not conducive to the public good'.[133]

Deportation Order

266. It should be noted that the Minister may, by executive instrument, order the deportation of a person on the terms and under the conditions that the Minster deems appropriate. If the Minister also deems it expedient to deport the dependants of the foreign national, he may so order.[134]

Effect of a Deportation Order

267. Regarding the effect of a deportation order, the law imposes an obligation on the deportee to observe the conditions of the order and to remain outside Ghana as long as the order is in force. Any person who disregards the conditions of his deportation order and enters Ghana commits an offence and is liable on summary conviction to a term of imprisonment not exceeding five years and may be deported without a further deportation order being made.

It is important to note that if a person against whom a deportation order has been made is already serving a prison sentence, that person shall complete his sentence unless the Minister otherwise directs.[135]

---

133. Section 35 Immigration Act, 2000 (Act 573).
134. Section 36 Immigration Act, 2000 (Act 573).
135. Section 37 Immigration Act, 2000 (Act 573).

Power to Arrest

268. A person who is yet to be deported and not under a supervision order may be arrested and detained under the authority of the Minister until that person is placed on board a vessel or aircraft by an immigration officer. [136]

Supervision Order

269. If a deportation order is not executed six months after it was made, the Minister may by executive order, make a supervision order requiring the foreign national to observe specific conditions pertaining to his place of residence and means of livelihood, the carrying on of political activities, reporting to an immigration officer and the police from time to time, and his association with persons with a criminal record. It is an offence to fail to comply with this supervision order and an offender is liable on summary conviction to a fine of no less than 250 penalty units or to a term of imprisonment of no less than two months or to both the fine and the term of imprisonment.

A deportation order is suspended while a supervision order is in force, but shall revive if the Minister so directs. In that case the supervision order ceases to have effect. Generally speaking, a supervision order expires two years from the date of the order and, on its expiration, the deportation order also expires.[137]

Expenses of Deportation

270. With regards to the financial implications of deportation, it is worth stressing that money or property belonging to the foreign national may be used to pay for the deportation expenses. A person who is connected with the bringing into Ghana of a prohibited immigrant is responsible for the deportation expenses of that person.[138]

136. Section 38 Immigration Act, 2000 (Act 573).
137. Section 40 Immigration Act, 2000 (Act 573).
138. Section 41 Immigration Act, 2000 (Act 573).

Chapter 2. Sanctions Against Persons Helping Illegal Entry and Residence

§1. Human Smuggling

271. Until 2012, Ghana did not have a specific law on human smuggling. The *Immigration (Amendment) Act, 2012 (Act 848*) as amended by the *Immigration Act, 2000 (Act 573*) provides for the offence of migrant smuggling. *Act 848* inserted section 52A entitled '*Prohibition of migrant smuggling*' into *Act 573*. Section 52A of *Act* 573 and *Act 848* provides that a person shall not engage in migrant smuggling. A person who does engage in migrant smuggling commits an offence and is liable on conviction to a fine of no less than 625 penalty units and no more than 1,250 penalty units, to a term of imprisonment for not less than five years and not more than ten years or to both.

272. Migrant smuggling is defined in section 52A of *Act 573* to mean 'the facilitation of the unlawful entry or departure from the country of a person in order to obtain, directly or indirectly, a financial or other material benefit'. 'Facilitation' is also defined in that section. It includes '*(a)* producing, procuring, providing or processing a travel or identity document by fraudulent means; *(b)* procuring by unlawful means other documentation in support of the processing of a travel or identity document; and *(c)* enabling a person who is not a national or a permanent resident to remain in the country without complying with the requirement for legally remaining in the country by any of the means mentioned in paragraphs *(a)* and *(b)*'. It appears that the prevention of human smuggling has been subsumed under the human trafficking laws of Ghana.

273. Section 52 of the *Immigration Act, 2000* (*Act 573*) makes it a criminal offence to help illegal immigrants or residents. It provides that a person commits an offence and is liable on conviction to a fine not exceeding 1,000 penalty units, to a term of imprisonment not exceeding two years or to both the fine and the term of imprisonment, if that person aids or assists a person to enter Ghana in contravention of *Act 573*; knowingly harbours a person whom the first mentioned knows is to be deported or has reasonable grounds to believe has acted in contravention of *Act 573*; knowingly permits or assists the escape from any vessel, aircraft or vehicle in Ghana of a person to be deported; disobeys or disregards an obligation imposed or order given by or under *Act 573*; knowingly makes or causes to be made a false return, false statement or false representation in connection with an obligation imposed or order given by or under Act *573*; restricts or obstructs an immigration officer in the execution of his duty; hinders or obstructs a deportation being effectuated under Act 573 wilfully and without lawful excuse; gives, sells or lends any registration certificate, card, passport or permit issued to that person under *Act 573* or any other act in order for it to be used by any other person; obtains or attempts to get a registration certificate, card, passport, permit or visa, or any other certificate for that person or any other person by false declaration; or, without lawful authority, uses or has in possession a forged certificate or card, passport, permit, visa or any other document or a passport, registration certificate or card or any other document on which any visa, photo or endorsement has been unlawfully affixed or altered.

274. When a master of a sea-going vessel, a master of an aircraft or a driver of a vehicle is charged with the offence of human trafficking, the clearance outwards of the vessel, aircraft or vehicle may be refused until the case has been heard and, on conviction, the fine imposed has been paid. Section 54 of *Act 573* provides that where a master of a vessel or a person in charge of an aircraft or a vehicle aids, abets or permits a person to disembark from that vessel, aircraft or vehicle or to leave the precincts of the port in contravention of any of the provisions of *Act 573*, the master or that person is liable to pay a penalty to the Immigration Service. If the master or that person fails to pay that penalty within fourteen days of demand, the master or that person commits an offence and is liable on summary conviction to a fine not exceeding 1,000 penalty units, to a term of imprisonment not exceeding two years, or to both the fine and the term of imprisonment. Thus individuals and/or carriers may be sanctioned and penalized for helping illegal immigrants or residents enter Ghana under the *Immigration Act, 2000 (Act 573)*. The *Human Trafficking Act, 2005 (Act 694)* also provides an elaborate legal framework to punish and penalize trafficking.

§2. Human Trafficking

275. The legal framework on the prevention, reduction and punishment of human trafficking and the rehabilitation and reintegration of trafficked persons is outlined in the *Human Trafficking Act, 2000 (Act 694)*. The law prescribes a minimum penalty of five-year imprisonment, but no maximum penalty, for all forms of trafficking. In February 2007, the first conviction of a trafficker was pronounced under *Act 694*. The convicted trafficker received a sentence of six years' imprisonment. In October 2006, the GIS created and staffed a position for a trafficking desk officer dedicated to overseeing anti-trafficking operations. Three Chinese traffickers were on Monday 22 June sentenced to a total of thirty-six years imprisonment with hard labour by an Accra Circuit Court presided over by Mrs Elizabeth Ankomah for trafficking women from China to Ghana. The Chinese women were recruited to work in a restaurant in Ghana, but upon their arrival in Ghana, their travel documents were taken from them and they were forced into sexual exploitation. The traffickers were arrested by the Ghana Anti-Trafficking Unit within the Criminal Investigations Department after an investigative journalist published a report on their activities.[139]

139. *See*, Gerald Dapaah Gyamfi, *International Responses to Human Trafficking: The Ghanaian Response*, Int'l J.Peace & Dev. Stud.65–66 (2016); *see also*, The Trafficking in Persons Report (2010), US State.

Department at 12; and New Crusading Guide, Chinese Traffickers in Tears over Jail Sentence (26 Jun. 2009) at https://www.modernghana.com/news/224063/chinese-traffickers-in-tears-over-jail-sentence.html.

276. The *Human Trafficking Act, 2005 (Act 694)* seeks to prevent, reduce and punish human trafficking. It creates, defines, prohibits and punishes trafficking offences and provides for rehabilitation and reintegration of trafficked persons and related matters. According to section 1 of *Act 694*, human trafficking is recruiting, transporting, transferring, harbouring or trading persons within and across national borders using threats, force, fraud, abuse of power, exploitation or financial incentives. Exploitation includes sexual exploitation, such as induced prostitution, forced labour, slavery and the removal of organs. Trafficking includes placement for sale, bonded or temporary placement, or placement where exploitation by someone else is the motivating factor. Where children are trafficked, neither the consent of the child nor its parents or guardian can be used as a defence in the proceedings even if the trafficker used fraud or deception, abuse of power or took advantage of the vulnerability of the child.[140]

Prohibition of Trafficking

277. Trafficking or acting as an intermediary for traffickers is a criminal offence punishable by a five-year maximum prison sentence. Acting as an intermediary involves participation in or facilitation of trafficking by someone who may or may not be known to the family of the trafficked person, such as sending, taking or agreeing, whether orally or in writing, to send or take someone to any place to be trafficked.[141]

Provision of Trafficked Person Prohibited

278. Providing another person for trafficking is a criminal offence even if the provider is a parent. Providing a person for trafficking purposes is a criminal offence punishable by a five-year maximum prison sentence.[142]

Use of Trafficked Persons Prohibited

279. Using a trafficked person is a criminal offence punishable by a five-year maximum prison sentence.[143]

Conveyance in Trafficking

280. Means of conveyance in trafficking includes conveyance by land, water or air.[144]

Duty to Inform

140. Section 1 of the Human Trafficking Act, 2005 (Act 694).
141. Section 2 of the Human Trafficking Act, 2005 (Act 694).
142. Section 3 of the Human Trafficking Act, 2005 (Act 694).
143. Section 4 of the Human Trafficking Act, 2005 (Act 694).
144. Section 5 of the Human Trafficking Act, 2005 (Act 694).

281. A person with information about trafficking must inform the police. In the alternative, that person can inform the Commission of Human Rights and Administrative Justice, the Department of Social Welfare, the Legal Aid Board or any reputable Civil Society Organisation of this fact. Failure to inform the police is a criminal offence punishable by a twelve-month maximum prison sentence, a fine of no less than 250 penalty units or both.[145]

Special Mitigating Factors

282. When a person is convicted of providing or using a trafficked person and the court finds that, due to special circumstances, the imposition of a minimum sentence in respect of the offence is harsh, it may impose a lower term of imprisonment plus a fine of no less than 500 penalty units.[146]

Application

283. A person may be tried and punished in Ghana for an act which, if done within the jurisdiction of the courts in this country, would constitute the offence of trafficking.[147]

Filing of Complaint to Police

284. A complaint may be filed by a victim or someone with information, where the victim or the offender resides, where the trafficking occurred or where the victim is residing temporarily. A social welfare officer, a probation officer, a health care provider, a teacher, a district labour officer may also file a complaint where intervention is in the best interest of the victim. A child may be assisted by a next friend when filing a complaint. Where a victim is, for any reason, unable to file a complaint, a member of his family or any person with knowledge of the offence may file a complaint on the victim's behalf. If the victim is deceased, the next-of-kin or any person with knowledge of the offence may file a complaint.[148]

Police Assistance

285. A police officer must respond and offer protection when trafficking is alleged even if the person making the report is not the victim. Failure to respond shall subject the police officer to a police service disciplinary procedure if a report is filed with his superior officer.[149]

Receipt of Complaint by Police

---

145. Section 6 of the Human Trafficking Act, 2005 (Act 694).
146. Section 7 of the Human Trafficking Act, 2005 (Act 694).
147. Section 8 of the Human Trafficking Act, 2005 (Act 694).
148. Section 9 of the Human Trafficking Act, 2005 (Act 694).
149. Section 10 of the Human Trafficking Act, 2005 (Act 694).

286. Upon receiving a complaint, the police officer shall take a detailed statement from the parties and witnesses and provide a copy to the victim, get the victim medical treatment and a place of safety where necessary and inform the victim of his/her rights and of any available material support. A next friend must be present when a statement is taken from a child.[150]

Arrest by Police

287. A warrant may be issued for the arrest of an alleged trafficker. However, he may also be arrested without a warrant where the act of trafficking is committed in the presence of a police officer, where he obstructs the execution of police duties or where he escapes or attempts to escape from lawful custody. A police officer may also arrest an alleged trafficker without a warrant where he has reasonable grounds to suspect that an alleged trafficker has committed or is about to commit the offence of trafficking and there is no other way to prevent the commission of the offence.[151]

Arrest by Private Person Without Warrant

288. A private person may arrest a person without a warrant if the person commits the act of trafficking in his presence or where he suspects that the offence of trafficking is about to be committed, the suspect must be handed over to the police immediately.[152]

Rescue of Trafficked Persons

289. An authorized officer in collaboration with an organization, or any government agency can rescue a trafficked person.[153]

Temporary Care and Counselling of Trafficked Person

290. Temporary basic material support and counselling services are provided by the Ministry through the District Assembly with resources from the Human Trafficking Fund. In these matters, the District Assembly must consult with the relevant government agencies and organizations in its area of authority.[154]

Tracing of Family of Trafficked Person

291. The Ministry is assisted by the police, an organization or any other person with information to trace the family of a trafficked person. It must consider the views of the trafficked person regarding reunification with his/her family. [155]

150. Section 11 of the Human Trafficking Act, 2005 (Act 694).
151. Section 12 of the Human Trafficking Act, 2005 (Act 694).
152. Section 13 of the Human Trafficking Act, 2005 (Act 694).
153. Section 14 of the Human Trafficking Act, 2005 (Act 694).
154. Sections 15 and 16 of the Human Trafficking Act, 2005 (Act 694).
155. Section 17 of the Human Trafficking Act, 2005 (Act 694).

Rehabilitation of Trafficked Person

292. The Ministry helps a rescued trafficking victim with employable skills to find employment or start-up capital. Financial assistance from the fund can be provided to trafficking victims. Rescue, rehabilitation and reintegration of a trafficked child are performed taking the best interest of the child into consideration.[156]

Compensation

293. A person convicted of trafficking is ordered to pay compensation to the trafficking victim. A person who causes injury to another during the act of trafficking can be ordered to pay compensation to the injured person. The payment of compensation does not detract from any other punishment that can be imposed of the trafficker.[157]

Establishment, Sources and Objective of Fund

294. The Human Trafficking Fund consists of voluntary contributions from individuals and organizations, money approved of by Parliament, grants from bilateral and multilateral sources, the proceeds from the confiscation of property connected with trafficking, and any other money approved by the Minister for Finance. The Human Trafficking Fund is used to pay basic material support, skills training, family tracing, rescue operations, rehabilitation, reintegration and the construction of reception shelters for trafficking victims. Persons connected with the rescue, rehabilitation and reintegration receive training and capacity building paid for from the Human Trafficking Fund.[158]

Management of and Payments from the Human Trafficking Fund

295. The Ministry has opened a bank account specifically for the Human Trafficking Fund and manages that fund. Payments made from the Human Trafficking Fund are done by cheque, signed by the Ministry accountant and any two of the Chief Directors of the Ministry, the secretary of the Management Board, or any other Management Board member nominated by the Board. The Management Board has developed guidelines for disbursements.[159]

Accounts and Audit and Annual Report

296. The Ministry keeps account books and proper records in the form approved by the Auditor-General and submits them for audit within three months of the end of the financial year. Within three months of receipt, the Auditor-General audits the

156. Section 18 of the Human Trafficking Act, 2005 (Act 694).
157. Section 19 of the Human Trafficking Act, 2005 (Act 694).
158. Sections 20–22 of the Human Trafficking Act, 2005 (Act 694).
159. Sections 23–24 of the Human Trafficking Act, 2005 (Act 694).

accounts and delivers a copy of the report to the Minister.[160] The financial year for the Human Trafficking Fund is the same as the financial year of the government. Within one month after the receipt of the audit report, the Minister submits to Parliament, an annual report covering the activities and operations of the Human Trafficking Fund that includes the audited accounts, the Auditor-General's report and any other information that the Minister considers necessary.[161]

297. A Human Trafficking Management Board has been established by the Human Trafficking Act which consists of the following persons:

(a) the chairperson, i.e., the Minister or Deputy Minister;
(b) one representative of the Attorney-General not below the level of Principal State Attorney;
(c) one representative of the Ministry of Local Government not below the level of a Deputy Director;
(d) one representative of the Ministry of Interior not below the level of a Deputy Director;
(e) one representative of the Ministry of Health not below the level of a Deputy Director;
(f) one representative of the Ministry of Education not below the level of a Deputy Director;
(g) one representative of the Ministry who acts as the secretary;
(h) one representative of the Ghana Journalists Association;
(i) one representative each from the:
  (1) Police Service.
  (2) Immigration Service.
  (3) Customs, Excise and Preventive Service.
  (4) the Office of the National Security Co-ordinator.
(j) the Director of Social Welfare;
(k) one representative of the Labour Department not below the level of a Deputy Chief Labour Officer;
(l) one person from the private sector nominated by the Minister; and
(m) three other persons, one of whom is a woman.

298. The members of the Human Trafficking Management Board other than the ex officio members are nominated by the institution they are employed by. The members of the Human Trafficking Management Board are appointed by the Minister with the authority of the President and must be committed to the fight against human trafficking.[162]

Functions of the Management Board

160. Section 25 of the Human Trafficking Act, 2005 (Act 694).
161. Section 27 of the Human Trafficking Act, 2005 (Act 694).
162. Section 29 of the Human Trafficking Act, 2005 (Act 694).

299. The Human Trafficking Management Board makes recommendations for a national plan of action against human trafficking and reports on its progress to the ECOWAS Secretariat through the Minister. They also advise the Minister on policy matters, provide assistance on investigation and prosecution of trafficking cases, and propose and promote strategies against trafficking in persons. Further, they liaise with government agencies and organizations to promote the rehabilitation and reintegration of victims of trafficking, prepare guidelines for disbursements from the Human Trafficking Fund and conduct research on international and regional developments and standards on trafficking in persons.[163]

Meetings of the Human Trafficking Management Board

300. The Human Trafficking Management Board meets at least once every three months with a quorum of five. The chairperson convenes and presides at meetings. In his absence, a member of the Human Trafficking Management Board elected by the members present shall preside the meeting. Matters are decided by a majority of the members present and voting. In the event of equality of votes, the person presiding has the deciding vote. The Human Trafficking Management Board may co-opt a person to attend their meetings, but the co-opted person may not vote on a matter up for decision by the Human Trafficking Management Board. The Human Trafficking Management Board determines the procedure for its meetings.[164]

Secretariat of the Human Trafficking Management Board

301. The Human Trafficking Management Board has a secretariat at the Ministry which provides the personnel and facilities for the performance of the Board's functions.[165]

Allowances

302. The Human Trafficking Management Board members are paid the allowances approved by the Minister in consultation with the Finance Minister.[166]

Continued Stay of Illegal Immigrants

303. A trafficked person who is in Ghana illegally may remain in the country throughout the investigation and prosecution of the trafficker. The Human Trafficking Management Board makes arrangements for the repatriation of the trafficked person at the end of the legal procedure. If it is in the best interest of the trafficked person, he may be allowed to remain in the country after the legal procedure has been completed. A trafficked person stays in a shelter provided by and with the approval of the Ministry of Interior and receives basic material support until he is

163. Section 30 of the Human Trafficking Act, 2005 (Act 694).
164. Section 31 of the Human Trafficking Act, 2005 (Act 694).
165. Section 32 of the Human Trafficking Act, 2005 (Act 694).
166. Section 33 of the Human Trafficking Act, 2005 (Act 694).

resettled. He may also be repatriated to his country of origin and stay in a reception centre at the Ministry's expense until such repatriation is effectuated.[167]

Extradition of Trafficking Offender

304. A non-citizen convicted of trafficking is deported.[168]

Power of Police under Act 30 and Act 560

305. The police powers given by Act 694 are in addition to the police powers provided under the *Criminal Procedure Code, 1960 (Act 30*) and the *Children's Act, 1998 (Act 560*).[169]

Reference to Family Tribunal

306. Where a child victim of trafficking needs care and protection, the court dealing with the trafficking offence may refer matters concerned with the child's needs to a Family Tribunal by virtue of the *Children's Act* of 1998.[170]

No Publication on Human Trafficking

307. No report on human trafficking proceedings that identifies a trafficked person is published unless the court provides leave to publish this information. Identifying a trafficked person without leave of the court is an offence punishable by a maximum twelve-month prison sentence, a fine of 250 penalty units or both.[171]

Criminal Charges and Civil Claim

308. In addition to the criminal charges arising from an act of human trafficking, the trafficking victim may also pursue a civil claim for damages against the trafficker.[172]

Confiscation of Property

309. Confiscation of property acquired with the gains from trafficking is ordered by the court, which may make appropriate orders in connection with the property and direct that the proceeds from its sale are paid into the Human Trafficking Fund.[173]

---

167. Section 34 of the Human Trafficking Act, 2005 (Act 694).
168. Section 35 of the Human Trafficking Act, 2005 (Act 694).
169. Section 36 of the Human Trafficking Act, 2005 (Act 694).
170. Section 37 of the Human Trafficking Act, 2005 (Act 694).
171. Section 38 of the Human Trafficking Act, 2005 (Act 694).
172. Section 39 of the Human Trafficking Act, 2005 (Act 694).
173. Section 40 of the Human Trafficking Act, 2005 (Act 694).

Regulations

310. The Minister may, by legislative instrument, adopt regulations containing preventive measures to be taken by District Assemblies against human trafficking; which include training of the security services to combat trafficking. He may also regulate the rescue and rehabilitation of trafficking victims and their reintegration by way of skills training and formal education. Further, he is empowered to regulate the collection of data and the exchange of information on human trafficking.[174]

174. Section 41 of the Human Trafficking Act, 2005 (Act 694).

Part VI. Legal Remedies and Procedural Safeguards

Chapter 1. Legal Remedies in Case of Refusal of Right to Enter, Stay or Reside

311. The right to enter Ghana is provided for in Article 21(1)(g) of Ghana's *1992 Constitution* as follows: 'all persons shall have the right to freedom of movement which means the right to move freely in Ghana, the right to leave and enter Ghana and immunity from expulsion from Ghana'. However, this right is not absolute. Article 21(4)(d) of the *1992 Constitution* claws back and derogates from it by permitting 'the imposition of restriction[s] on the freedom of entry into Ghana, or movement in Ghana, of a person who is not a citizen of Ghana'. Any such restriction must be done under the authority of a law and must be reasonably justifiable in terms of the spirit of the Constitution. The spirit and letter of Article 296 of the *1992 Constitution* supports this. This provision provides that a person or authority vested with discretionary power has a duty to be fair and candid, and the exercise of discretionary power may not be used arbitrary, capricious or biased either by resentment, prejudice or personal dislike, and shall be in accordance with due process of law and published regulations. Moreover, Article 23 of the *1992 Constitution* of Ghana provides that 'Administrative bodies and administrative officials shall act fairly and reasonably and comply with the requirements imposed on them by law, and persons aggrieved by the exercise of such acts and decisions shall have the right to seek redress before a court or other tribunal.' Thus all persons have the right to appeal against a refusal of their right to enter Ghana.Sections 46 and 47 of the *Immigration Act, 2000 (Act 573)* provide for this as follows.

Submission of Petitions

312. With the exception of a prohibited immigrant, a person aggrieved by the revocation of his permit to stay in Ghana, the refusal to grant or renew his permit, or a repatriation ordered by an immigration officer may petition the appropriate Minister within seven days of the adoption of that decision requesting him to re-evaluate the offending act. The Minister reassesses the decision with the assistance of a committee composed of a representative of the Attorney-General not below the rank of a Senior State Attorney, who shall be the chairman of the com mittee; a representative of the Minister for Foreign Affairs not below the rank of a Director; and one other person appointed by the Minister who is not an officer or employee of the Immigration Service.

313. It must be emphasized that a foreign national cannot petition the Minister in respect of a deportation order issued under an executive instrument and signed by the Minister.[175]

Petition Not to Act as Stay of Action

314. A petition made to the Minister by a foreign national does not stay the offending act, though regulations may provide the conditions determining when a person may be permitted to stay in Ghana pending the hearing of a petition made by that person.[176]

315. Prohibited immigrants are barred from entering Ghana, and section 8(2) of *Act 573* provides that 'a person who enters Ghana while a prohibited immigrant commits an offence and is liable on summary conviction to a fine not exceeding five hundred penalty units or to a term of imprisonment of not less than six months and not exceeding two years or to both the fine and the imprisonment'. However, even such person has a right of appeal. Section 8(3) of *Act 573* provides that 'where a person is charged with an offence under Section 8(2), the burden of proof that that person is not a prohibited immigrant lies on that person'. Section 51 of *Act 573* vests the Minister with 'Residual Powers' where the Minister may revoke or *waive* a visa, permit, condition of entry and any other requirement on grounds of national interest, compassionate circumstances, or any other reasonable ground.

316. Under section 15(3) of *Act 573*, 'where a person is granted an indefinite residence status and that person is absent from Ghana for more than twelve consecutive months, the indefinite resident status is automatically lost'. Section 15(4) of *Act 573* empowers 'a person who loses an indefinite residence status under Section 15(3) *Act 573* to apply to the Director for reinstatement, but the application shall be treated as a fresh application subject to the conditions determined by the Director'. Section 16(3) and (4) *Act 573* contains similar rules for a foreign spouse regarding automatic loss of a residence right and an application for reinstatement. Articles 23 and 33 of the *1992 Constitution* also provide detailed remedies and procedures for the enforcement of human rights and revision of administrative decisions.

317. The legal remedies against expulsion usually follow the petition procedure in sections 46, 47 and 51 of *Act 573* as discussed *supra* in paragraphs 313–315. Also, all persons have a right to appeal to the courts. This right is guaranteed by Article 23 of the *1992 Constitution* of Ghana as follows: 'administrative bodies and administrative officials shall act fairly and reasonably and comply with the require

175. Section 46 of the Immigration Act, 2000 (Act 573).
176. Section 47 of the Immigration Act, 2000 (Act 573).

ments imposed on them by law, and persons aggrieved by the exercise of such acts and decisions shall have the right to seek redress before a court or other tribunal'.

318. Article 33 of the 1992 Constitution provides access to the High Court to redress in any case where a person's fundamental human rights have been violated, as set out in the Constitution. Such a person, if aggrieved with the High Court's decision, may appeal to the Court of Appeal and further to the Supreme Court (Article 33 of the *1992 Constitution*).

319. Section 34(1) of the *Human Trafficking Act, 2005 (Act 694)*provides that, notwithstanding the provisions in section 21 of the *Immigration Act, 2000 (Act 573)* (on the removal of an illegal immigrant), a trafficked person who is in Ghana unlawfully, may remain in Ghana throughout the period of a legal investigation and prosecution of a trafficker. The Human Trafficking Management Board makes the arrangements for the repatriation of the trafficked person upon completion of the legal process. Under section 3 of the *Refugees Law, 1992 (PNDCL 305D)*, a refugee may be detained or expelled for reasons of national security or public order, However, no refugee may be expelled to a country where he has reason to fear persecution.

Chapter 2. Legal Remedies in Case of Detention

320. Ghana's *Habeas Corpus Act, 1964 (Act 244)* provides that where an allegation is made by any person that he is being detained unlawfully, an application may be made to the High Court or any Judge of the High Court for an enquiry into the case of detention. Under section 1 of *Act 244,* such an application may be made by the person alleging that he is being detained unlawfully; any person entitled to the custody of the person detained; or any other person acting on behalf of the person detained. The application is made in writing and must contain the name and description of the person detained; the place of detention; the mode and manner of arrest; and any other particulars the applicant may wish to bring before the High Court. The Court must make enquiries into the allegation of unlawful detention immediately and may make an order requiring the person in whose custody the applicant is detained to present the person so detained before the High Court on a day specified in the order and to submit a report in writing stating the grounds of the detention.

321. Pursuant to section 4 of the Habeas Corpus *Act, 1964 (Act 244)*, the High Court shall, upon presentation of the person being detained before it and after giving the person whose custody he is detained an opportunity to justify the detention measure, order the release of the person detained unless the High Court is satisfied that the detention is in accordance with law. All appeals relating to Habeas Corpus applications are dealt with by the Supreme Court and not by the Court of Appeal. Depending on the circumstances of the appeal or reference to the Supreme Court, the person detained may be allowed by the Supreme Court to be released on bail on such conditions as it deems fit until the question referred to it has been decided.

322. Undersection 7(1) of *Act 573*, where an immigration officer is in doubt as to the right of a person to enter Ghana, the officer may send that person to be detained, and that person shall remain in custody pending the determination of the matter. However, a person so detained may appeal to the Director of Immigration under section 7(2) of *Act 573*, and the Director may, pending the completion of enquiries in respect of the detained person, release him from custody on directions determined by the Director and may for that purpose issue a temporary permit to that person.

Part VII. Access to the Labour Market

Chapter 1. Overview of Applicable Legislation

323. Some of the relevant legislative acts on immigrant labour market access are the Immigration Act, 2000 (Act 573), Immigration Regulations, 2001 (L.I. 1697), GIPC Act, 2013 (Act 865), Free Zones Act, 1995 (Act 504), Labour Regulations, 2007 (L.I. 1833), etc. The main legislative act is the Immigration Act, 2000 (Act 573). Sections 24–34 of the Immigration Act, 2000 contain relevant provisions on the employment of foreign nationals in accordance with an immigrant quota. It also provides for the calculation of the immigrant quota, work permits for foreign immigrants, guarantees to be provided by and obligations of both the employer and the foreign employee.

324. Sections 24–26 of the *Immigration Act, 2000 (Act 573)* provide for the establishment of an Immigrant Quota Committee consisting of the Deputy Minister, who is the chairman, the Director of Immigration or the representative of the Director not below the position of a Deputy Director, and one representative each from the Ministries of the Interior, Employment and Social Welfare, Trade and Industry, the Registrar General's Department, the Ghana Investments Promotion Centre, the Bank of Ghana, the Statistical Service and the Ghana Employers Association. The Ministry of the Interior representative is the secretary to the Immigrant Quota Committee.

325. A foreign national shall not be employed in Ghana except in accordance with a permit granted by the Immigrant Quota Committee. This Committee considers applications for immigrant quotas and work permits, guided by the country's relevant investment laws and submits its recommendations to the Minister. Work permits shall be issued to persons who are not prohibited immigrants, visitors, tourists, transit passengers or students. The Committee issues a work permit if it is satisfied that an applicant for a work permit is qualified to work or undertake employment in the trade, business or calling in respect of which the application is made and wishes to enter Ghana in order to take up work or employment in such trade or business or is lawfully resident in Ghana and, finally, that the taking up of the work or employment will benefit Ghana generally.

326. A work permit for the employment of a foreign national specifies the number and description of persons authorized to be employed and the employer. The holder of the permit may not engage in any form of paid employment, business or professional occupation in Ghana, other than that specified in the work permit. An approval to fill an immigrant quota may specify the period during which a foreign national may fill a particular position while a citizen understudies the foreign national with a view to take over the position on the expiry of the specified period in the work permit. According to section 32 of *Act 573*, an application for the renewal of a work permit shall be made a month before the permit is due to expire; this application is treated as a fresh application.

327. When a foreign national starts work in Ghana, he and his employer have seven days each to notify the Immigrant Quota Committee of the commencement date. A copy in the prescribed form has to be sent to the Director of Immigration. The employer must also provide the Director with a letter of guarantee in respect of any repatriation expenses of the foreign national.

When a foreign national ceases to work in Ghana, he and his employer have seven days each to notify the Immigrant Quota Committee of such cessation. A copy of the prescribed form is to be sent to the Director. The employer must comply with the directions of the Director as to the arrangements for the repatriation of the foreign national and his dependants, where appropriate.

328. Under section 31 of *Act 573*, no later than the January 15, of every year, a person to whom an immigrant quota is granted must send the Committee, with a copy for the Director, an annual return stating the names and addresses of the foreign nationals employed by that person in Ghana on January 1 of that year. Any corporate body that fails to do so is liable to pay a penalty. Any individual who fails to do so is also liable to pay a penalty. Failure to pay the prescribed penalty within seven days is an offence punishable by a six-month to two-year prison sentence, a fine of 500 penalty units or both. The term of imprisonment applies only to individuals.

329. Section 33 of *Act 573* provides that an employer's letter of guarantee in respect of the repatriation of a foreign national makes him liable to pay repatriation expenses if the foreign national ceases to work for him as well as any repatriation expenses incurred by the repatriation of the dependants of the foreign national in the event of the death of the latter. The employer may be released from the guarantee if the Director is satisfied that alternative security for any repatriation expenses caused by a foreign national and his dependants has been provided or in the event that they have left Ghana.

330. Foreign nationals who remain in Ghana longer than three months must register with the nearest immigration office. Failure to do so is an offence punishable by a maximum twelve-month prison sentence, a fine of 250 penalty units or both.

331. The *Immigration Regulations, 2001 (L.I. 1697)* contain very important provisions on the employment of foreign nationals. The *Immigration Regulations of 2001* provide that an employer who wishes to apply for a work permit for an employee must submit an application through the Director of Immigration, who, upon investigation, submits a report to the Immigrant Quota Committee for consid eration and approval.[177]Corporate bodies and individuals who employ foreigners without work permits have to pay the specified penalties to the Immigration Service. Failure to pay this penalty within seven days is an offence punishable by a fine of 700 penalty units and 350 penalty units, respectively.[178]

332. Section 27 of the *Immigration Act, 2000 (Act 573)* sets out the functions of the Immigrant Quota Committee. It provides that the Immigrant Quota Committee is to be guided when considering an application for an immigrant quota and work permit *by the relevant investment laws of the country*. Two main legislative acts on investment are applicable in this context: (1) The *GIPC Act, 2013 (Act 865)* and (2) the *Free Zones Act, 1995 (Act 504)*. In recognition of the work of the GIPC, Free Zones Board, etc., section 29 of *Act 573* reserves the existing rights of other bodies to grant immigrant quotas as follows: 'without prejudice to the generality of Section 27, a relevant body granting immigrant quotas under any other enactment shall continue to exercise that authority subject to this Act'. Section 27 of *Act 865* reserves certain activities for Ghanaians exclusively (*see* paragraph 40). Section 28 of *Act 865* requires foreign capital investment for foreign enterprises in Ghana (*see* paragraph 41 *supra*). Section 35 of *Act 865* provides *immigrant quotas* based on the paid-up capital of a foreign enterprise (*see* paragraph 42).

333. The *Free Zones Act, 1995 (Act 504)*, as amended by the *Free Zone (Amendment) Act, 2002 (Act 618)*, provides for the establishment of free zones to aid economic development. It provides for the regulation of activities in free zones and related matters. It focuses on the promotion of investment in the manufacturing sector especially with an aim of exporting the bulk of the products and provides for the participation of foreign investors in the Free Zones. Section 29 of *Act 504* states that: (1) a foreign investor may take and hold a maximum of 100% of the shares in a free zone enterprise; (2) a domestic investor may take and hold a maximum of 100% of the shares in an export free zone enterprise; and (3) foreign and domestic investors have equal status within the export free zones. However, section 12 of *Act 504* provides that a person shall not carry on a trade, business or industry within a free zone unless it is registered under (a)the *Companies Act, 1963 (Act 179)*, or (b) the *Incorporated Private Partnerships Act, 1962 (Act 152)*, and is the holder of an incorporated licence authorizing the carrying on of that trade, business or industry under *Act 504*.

334. Section 34 of the *Free Zones Act, 1995 (Act 504)* (as substituted by Free Zone (Amendment) Act, 2002 (Act 618)) deals with employment in Free Zones. Free zone developers and enterprises are free to negotiate and establish contracts of employment with employees that include wage scales, minimum working hours, employee suspension and dismissal, settlement of disputes arising between employers and employees, and any other terms of employment if consistent with I.L.O. Conventions on worker's rights and conditions of service. Work and resident permits are required for any foreign national who wishes to live in Ghana and work in

177. Regulation 16 Immigration Regulations, 2001 (L.I. 1697).
178. Regulation 18 Immigration Regulations, 2001 (L.I. 1697).

a free zone. Application for work and resident permits for foreign employees of free zone enterprises are submitted to the Free Zones Board which takes the necessary action in consultation with the Immigration Service. Section 34 of *Act 592* also provides that a foreign employee must pay the appropriate tax to the Government of Ghana on any income earned in Ghana, including income earned in the free zone during that period of work in accordance with existing income tax legislation and subject to the provisions in any double taxation agreement between the Government of Ghana and the Government of which the foreign employee is a national.

335. The *Concessions Act (Ordinance), 1939 (Cap 136)* also contains provisions on migrant workers. Section 34(1) of *Cap 136* is entitled *Mining Leases* and provides: 'An alien shall not carry on mining unless the alien is the holder of (a) a concession granting the right to do so from a citizen having the power to grant that right; and (b) a mining licence from the Minerals Commission ... or where the mining is conducted solely by dredging operations, an appropriate dredging licence under the Rivers Act'. Section 19(4) of the *Small Scale Gold Mining Law, 1989 (PNDCL 218)*, provides that 'where an alien is convicted of an offence under this Act the alien is liable, after paying of the fine or serving the imprisonment imposed, to deportation (under the *Immigration Act, 2000 (Act 573)*)'. The *Diamonds Act, 1972 (N.R.C.D. 32)* has similar provisions in its section 13 entitled '*Alien offender liable to deportation*': 'Where an alien is convicted of an offence under this Act, the alien is, after paying the fine or serving the sentence, liable to deportation under section 36 of the *Immigration Act, 2000 (Act 573)*.'

336. Regulation 51(4) of the *Social Security Regulations, 1973 (L.I. 818)* provides that 'an alien employer may not be permitted to leave Ghana unless he produces to the appropriate immigration authorities a valid Social Security Clearance Certificate issued in respect of his establishment'. The *Internal Revenue Act, 2000 (Act 592)* provides for '*Tax clearance certificates*' in section 118 as follows: 'an alien who has been resident in the Republic or who, not being a person so resident, has a tax liability due under this Act or has income which accrued in or was derived from the Republic with respect to which that alien is chargeable to tax under Sections 1- 94 of *Act 592*, shall not depart from the Republic unless that alien produces to the immigration officer at the port of departure a tax clearance certificate'.

337. The *Labour Regulations, 2007 (L.I. 1833)* also contain several provisions on employment of foreigners and relevant related matters, more specifically, Regulations 21–37. Regulations 21–22 prohibit the employment of children or human trafficking victims. Human trafficking is explained in section 1 of the Human Trafficking Act, 2005 (Act 694) and discussed in paragraph 276. According to Regulation 23 of *L.I. 1833*, consent is not a defence to justify the act of trafficking. So where children are trafficked, neither the consent of the child nor its parents or guardian can be used as a defence in the prosecution of a trafficker if the trafficker used fraud or deception, abuse of power, or took advantage of the vulnerability of the child. (*see also* section 1(4) of Act 694).

338. Regulations 24 and 25 of L.I. 1833 essentially restate the law as provided in sections 2 and 3 of Act 694 and discussed in paragraphs 277 and 278, respectively. Regulation 26 of L.I. 1833 stipulates that using the services of a trafficked person is a criminal offence punishable by a five-year maximum prison sentence. (*see* section 4 of Act 694).

339. Regulation 27 of the *Labour Regulations, 2007 (L.I. 1833)* deals with foreign employment and provides that where a worker is re-engaged in a foreign contract and the total period of service involves separation from his family for more than eighteen months, he may not begin the re-engagement until he has had the opportunity to return home at the expense of the employer. Regulation 28 of *L.I.1833* forests out the conditions for foreign employment: The Chief Labour Officer ensures that employers do not engage workers under foreign contracts. This does not apply to sea-going vessels unless the service is provided in one of the countries specified in a notice under the regulations. Countries to which immigration of workers is lawful may also be specified in a notice. A person who is under 18 years of age may not be employed under a foreign contract. A foreign contract is valid for a period of one year from the date of execution or for two years with permission in writing from the Chief Labour Officer.

340. A copy of each foreign contract must be forwarded by the Chief Labour Officer to the Ministries of Foreign Affairs, Interior and Manpower Youth and Employment of the country where the contract duties are to be discharged. When a foreign contract is entered into, the employer must pay a capitation fee, determined by the Minister in consultation with the Chief Labour Officer, to the Chief Labour Officer, or a Labour Officer in respect of each worker. The Chief Labour Officer ascertains the genuineness of the employment offer before signing the contract. The Chief Labour Officer or a Labour Officer who attests to a foreign contract furnishes the Director of Immigration or an Immigration Officer at the port of embarkation, or place of departure with the name of the worker engaged.

341. An employer may not assign a contract without the consent of the worker and the Chief Labour Officer or the Labour Officer's endorsement. The Labour Officer must ascertain that the worker's consent has not been obtained by coercion, undue influence, misrepresentation or mistake; otherwise the contract may be declared void by the worker. Under Regulation 33 of *L.I. 1833*, an employer may not use fraud, falsehood, intimidation, coercion or misrepresentation to induce another person to enter into a foreign contract. If this is the case, the contract is void. Such an employer must pay the repatriation expenses of the worker and his family if he has been taken to the place of employment by the employer.

342. Regulation 31 of *L.I. 1833* provides that a worker employed under a foreign contract has the right to be accompanied by his family during the period of employment. His employment may not be considered to include the recruitment of any member of his family. The family members who can accompany him are: the spouse and children under the age of 16. No member of the worker's family may be prevented from accompanying the worker or be separated from him after accom panying him to his place of employment except at the express request of the person concerned. According to Regulation 34 of *L.I. 1833*, an employee under a foreign contract shall have his and his family's travel expenses to the place of employment, including expenses for protection during the journey, paid by the employer. These expenses include the necessaries for the journey and for repatriation.

343. According to Regulation 32 of *L.I. 1833*, where the Chief Labour Officer or a Labour Officer considers it necessary, summaries of the law relating to a contract may be printed in English and any local language and placed in prominent places on the employer's premises for the employee's benefit. An employer who fails to comply with such a request from the Chief Labour Officer or Labour Officer commits an offence.

344. According to Regulation 35 of L.I. 1833, where an employer is unable to fulfil the contract, or where the employee, due to illness or an accident, is unable to fulfil the contract, the contract may be terminated by either party. The worker is entitled to any earned and deferred pay and compensation due in respect of sickness or accident, and repatriation for himself and his family, unless the contract provides otherwise. A contract may be terminated by agreement between the parties if a Labour Officer has approved the agreement after certifying that the worker's consent was not obtained by coercion, undue influence, misrepresentation or mistake, and that monetary liabilities between the parties have been satisfied. Where the Chief Labour Officer gives prior approval to the agreement, the worker may terminate the contract on the ground of ill-treatment by the employer. The death of the employee terminates the contract, but does not prejudice the legal rights of the employee's heirs or dependants.

345. Regulations 36 and 37 of *L.I. 1833* are on repatriation. An employee engaged under a foreign contract and the members of his family who have been authorized to accompany him to the place of employment are repatriated at the expense of the employer where the employee becomes sick or has an accident during the journey to the place of employment; where the employee is found to be medically unfit for employment; where the term of employment expires; where the employment ends due to the inability of the employer to fulfil the undertakings in the contract; where the employment ends due to the inability of the employee to fulfil the undertakings of the contract owing to sickness or accident; where the employment ends by mutual agreement between the employer and the worker unless the agreement provides otherwise; where the employment is ended by the employer or the employee where the Chief Labour Officer or a Labour Officer directs so in writing, or if any other reason occurs in the course of the worker's employment. An employer who fails to repatriate an employee or his family under these circumstances commits an offence.

346. The employer may, however, be exempted from the payment of repatriation expenses if the Chief Labour Officer or a Labour Officer is satisfied that the employee has verbally or in writing, declined the right to repatriation and accepted settlement at or near the place of employment. The employer is also exempted from the payment of repatriation expenses if the employee fails to exercise the right to repatriation within three months of the termination of the employment or if the employment was terminated as a result of the fault of the employee, subject to the approval of a Labour Officer. If repatriation is delayed by choice of the employee, the employer is not responsible for his subsistence during the period from the end of the employment term until the date of repatriation.

Chapter 2. Conditions for Entitlement to Work in the Country as an Employed Person

§1. General Conditions

347. Foreign nationals need a work permit that enables them to work in Ghana. A work permit is normally granted by the Minister of Interior after the foreign national has satisfied the Immigrant Quota Committee that he satisfies various conditions including that:

- the person is not a prohibited immigrant;
- the person is not a student, visitor, tourist or transit passenger;
- he wishes to enter Ghana in order to take up work or employment;
- he is qualified to work or undertake employment in the trade, business or calling in respect of which the application was made;
- his taking up of the work or employment generally benefits Ghana;
- he is lawfully resident in Ghana and is qualified to work as an employee; and
- it is not employment in an enterprise reserved for Ghanaians under the Schedule to section 27 of the *GIPC Act, 2013 (Act 865*), (*see* paragraph 40 *supra*).

§2. Administrative Rules and Procedures

348. Section 24 of the *Immigration Act, 2000 (Act 573*) makes it mandatory for all foreign nationals who seek work in Ghana to be employed in accordance with a work permit granted by the Immigrant Quota Committee. The *Immigration Regulations, 2001 (L.I. 1697*) detail the procedure for employing foreign nationals (Regulations 16–18) as follows.

Employment of Foreign Nationals

349. An application to employ a foreign national must be made through the Director of Immigration, who, upon investigations, submits a report to the Immigrant Quota Committee for consideration. The Immigrant Quota Committee in turn submits its recommendations to the sector Minister for the issuing or denial of the work permit. The format of the work permit that is issued to a successful applicant is found in the Schedule to the Regulations and is labelled, Form L.[179]

Notification to the Immigrant Quota Committee

350. The Immigrant Quota Committee must be informed by the employer of changes in the status of his foreign employee. For instance, the Immigrant Quota Committee must be notified when the employee starts work and when he ceases to be an employee. The forms required for giving such notices are also found in the

179. Regulation 16 of the Immigration Regulations, 2001 (L.I. 1697) and s. 23 of Act 573.

Schedule to the Regulations and are designated, Forms M, N, O, P, Q. The form of the annual return, as required by section 31(1) of the *Immigration Act,* is also included in the Schedule and is labelled, Form R.[180]

Penalty for Illegal Employment

351. All applications to employ a foreign national must be in accordance with the provisions of the *Immigration Act.* A corporate body that employs a foreigner in breach of the provisions of section 24 of the *Immigration Act,* that is, in accordance with a permit granted by the Immigrant Quota Committee, must pay the Immigration Service a penalty. An individual employer, who does not comply with section 24 of the *Immigration Act,* is also liable to pay a penalty. A corporate body that fails to pay the prescribed penalty within seven days of being notified commits an offence and is liable on summary conviction to pay a fine of 700 penalty units. An individual who fails to pay the prescribed penalty also commits an offence and is liable on summary conviction to pay a fine of 350 penalty units.[181]

352. The general guidelines on the administrative requirements or procedure for the employment of foreign immigrants (as gleaned from the provisions of *Immigration Act, 2000 (Act 573*) especially sections 24–34) may be summed up as follows:

(a) No foreigner shall employ or accept employment in Ghana unless that person is granted a work permit or Immigrant quota.
(b) A work permit or Immigrant quota is an authorization granted to an employer or employee to engage in lawful and gainful employment in Ghana.
(c) A work permit or Immigrant quota specifies the job title and indicates the employer by whom that person is employed and the holder cannot engage in any other employment, business, profession or occupation in Ghana for reward than what is specified in the work permit or the Immigrant quota.
(d) Foreign spouses with special skills may, on application to the Minister of Interior, be issued with work permits to work as long as they remain with their partner who enjoy a lawful residential status in Ghana.
(e) A foreigner who has been granted a work permit or Immigrant quota cannot start working immediately in Ghana unless that person has been issued a residence permit by the Director of Immigration that allows him to remain and work in the country.
(f) When a foreign national begins to work for an employer in Ghana, the employer has to give notice to the issuing authority of a work permit or an Immigrant quota no later than seven days after the commencement of employment in the prescribed form, indicating the commencement date and a copy has to be sent to the Director of Immigration. A letter of guarantee in respect of repatriation expenses of the employee should also be submitted to the Director.

180. Regulation 17 of the Immigration Regulations, 2001 (L.I. 1697).
181. Regulation 18 of the Immigration Regulations, 2001 (L.I. 1697).

(g) Similarly, the employee has to give notice of the commencement date to the issuing authority no later than seven days after the commencement of employment and a copy has to be sent to the Director of immigration.

(h) If a foreign national ceases to work in Ghana the employer has to give notice of the cessation no later than seven days after the cessation to the issuing authority and a copy has to be sent to the Director of immigration. The employer has to comply with the directions of the Director as to the arrangements for the repatriation of the employee and his dependants, if any. The employee also has to notify the Director.

(i) An individual or body corporate to whom a work permit or an Immigrant quota has been granted, is obliged to submit annual returns, no later than the fourteenth day of January of each year to the issuing authority and a copy has to be sent to the Director of immigration, stating the names and addresses of all foreign employees in their employment as of 1 January. Other particulars which may be requested will also have to be provided.

(j) An employer is liable to pay all repatriation expenses of an employee and his dependants if the employee ceases to work for the employer and repatriation becomes necessary.

§3. Conditions for Special Categories of Workers

353. Section 12 of the *Free Zones Act, 1995 (Act 504)* provides that a person shall not carry on a trade, business or industry within a free zone unless it is registered under (a) the *Companies Act, 1963 (Act 179)*, or (b) *Incorporated Private Partnerships Act, 1962 (Act 152)*, and is the holder of an incorporated licence authorizing the carrying on of that trade, business or industry under the *Free Zones Act, 1995 (Act 504)*. The Free Zones Act provides administrative requirements and procedures in section 34 (as substituted by *Free Zone (Amendment) Act, 2002 (Act 618)*). Free zone developers and enterprises are free to negotiate and establish contracts of employment with employees that include wage scales, minimum working hours, employee suspension and dismissal, settlement of disputes arising between employers and employees, and any other terms of employment if consistent with I.L.O. Conventions on worker's rights and conditions of service.

354. Work and resident permits are required for any foreign national who wishes to live in Ghana and work in a free zone. Applications for work and resident permits for foreign employees of free zone enterprises are submitted to the Free Zones Board which takes the necessary action in consultation with the Immigration Service. A foreign employee must pay the appropriate tax to the Government of Ghana on any income earned in Ghana, including income earned in the free zone during that period of work, in accordance with existing income tax legislation and subject to the provisions of any double taxation agreement between the Government of Ghana and the Government of which the foreign employee is a national. Section 29 of the *Free Zones Act, 1995 (Act 504)* states that a foreign investor may take and hold a maximum of 100% of the shares in a free zone enterprise; a domestic inves tor may take and hold a maximum of 100% of the shares in an export free zone enterprise; and foreign and domestic investors have equal status within the export free zones.

355. The Ghana *Investment Promotion Act, 2013 (Act 865)* provides a clear and stable institutional framework for foreign investors. Section 27 of *Act 865* reserves many activities for Ghanaians (*see* paragraph 40 *supra*). Section 28 of *Act 865* provides that an enterprise in which foreign participation is permitted, may not be established or operated by a person who is not a citizen of Ghana unless certain foreign capital investment requirements are met (*see* paragraph 41 *supra*). Section 35 of *Act 865* provides for varying immigrant quotas based on the amount of paid-up capital for a foreign enterprise (*see* paragraph 42 *supra*). An enterprise that intends to employ an expatriate must apply to the GIPC for facilitation of the employment. The application must specify the number of expatriates to be employed. An application submitted under this section is dealt with by the Immigration Service in consultation with the GIPC.

356. Section 34(1) of the *Concessions Act (Ordinance), 1939 (Cap 136)* has the following provisions on migrants. Entitled *Mining Leases*, it provides that 'An alien shall not carry on mining unless the alien is the holder of (a) a concession granting the right to do so from a citizen having the power to grant that right; and (b) a mining licence from the Minerals Commission ... or where the mining is conducted solely by dredging operations, an appropriate dredging licence under the Rivers Act'. The *Minerals and Mining Act, 2006 (Act 703*) also provides for the acquisition of mineral rights. According to section 9(1) and (2) of *Act 703,* notwithstanding a right or title which a person may have to land in, upon or under which minerals are situated, a person shall not conduct activities on or over land in Ghana for the search, reconnaissance, prospecting, exploration or mining for a mineral unless that person has been granted a mineral right in accordance with *Act 703*. Activities conducted under a mineral right are limited to the activities permitted by the mineral right.

357. Under section 10 of *Act 703*, unless otherwise provided in that Act, a mineral right is not granted to a person, unless that person is a body incorporated under the *Companies Code 1963 (Act 179*), under the *Incorporated Private Partnerships Act 1962 (Act 152*) or under an enactment in force. Section 11 of *Act 703* governs applications for a mineral right, and every application must be submitted to the Minerals Commission in the prescribed form and accompanied by a statement providing, (a) the particulars of the financial and technical resources available to the applicant for the proposed mineral operations, (b) an estimate of the amount of money proposed to be spent on the operations, (c) the particulars of the programme for proposed mineral operations, and (d) the particulars of the applicant's proposals with respect to the employment and training in the mining industry of Ghanaians.

358. There are some provisions in the *Refugees Law, 1992 (PNDCL 305D*) setting out the conditions for refugees to takeup wage-earning employment. Article 17(3) of the 1951 UN Convention Relating to Status of Refugees (which has been incorporated into *PNDCL 305D* by section 11 and the Schedule to *PNDCL 305D*) provides that 'Contracting States shall give sympathetic consideration to assimilating the rights of all refugees with regard to wage-earning employment to those of nationals, and in particular of those refugees who have entered their territory pursuant to programmes of labour recruitment or under immigration schemes'.

Chapter 3. Sanctions Against Illegal Participation in the Labour Market

§1. Sanctions Against Employers

359. Regulation 18 of the *Immigration Regulations, 2001(L.I. 1697)* provides some sanctions against an employer who breaches the rules on employment of foreign nationals. First, it provides that a person shall not employ a foreigner except in accordance with the provisions of the *Immigration Act.* Anybody corporate or individual who employs a foreigner in breach of the provisions of section 24 of the *Immigration Act* (employs a foreign national in Ghana without a permit granted by the Immigrant Quota Committee) must pay a penalty to the Immigration Service. A body corporate which fails to pay the prescribed penalty within seven days commits an offence and is liable on summary conviction to pay a fine of 700 penalty units and any individual who fails to pay the prescribed penalty commits an offence and is liable on summary conviction to pay a fine of 350 penalty units.

360. Section 31 of the *Immigration Act, 2000 (Act 573)* entitled '*Annual returns*' provides that not later than fourteen days after the January 1, of each year, a person to whom an immigrant quota has been granted under that Act or any other enactment, must submit to the Committee, with a copy to the Director, an annual return in the prescribed form stating the names and addresses of the foreign nationals employed by that person in Ghana as of the January 1 of that year and provide any other particulars which may be prescribed. A body corporate or individual who fails to comply with this obligation is liable to pay the Immigration Service a penalty. A body corporate or an individual who fails to pay the prescribed penalty within seven days, commits an offence and is liable on summary conviction to a fine of 500 penalty units, a term of imprisonment of no less than six months and no more than two years or to both the fine and the term of imprisonment. The latter only applies to the individual, not to a body corporate.

§2. Sanctions Against Workers

361. Regulation 38 of the *Labour Regulations, 2007 (L.I. 1833)* provides as follows:

(1) A person who contravenes any of these regulations commits an offence and is liable on summary conviction to a fine of twenty-five penalty units.
(2) Where a body corporate commits an offence under these Regulations:
  (a) every director of the body corporate is considered to have committed that offence unless the director proves that the offence was committed without the directors consent or connivance or that the director exercised due diligence to prevent the commission of the offence as the director ought to have exercised having regard to the nature of the director's functions and circumstances; and

(b) in the case of a partnership or a firm every partner of the partnership or firm shall be considered to have committed that offence.

362. Section 21 of the Immigration Act, 2000 (Act 573) entitled 'Removal of illegal immigrants' provides as follows:

(1) Where the presence of a person in Ghana is unlawful, that person may be repatriated from Ghana by an order of the Director.
(2) Where a person is ordered to be removed from Ghana under this Act, that person may be arrested and detained for a period that is necessary for making arrangements for the removal.
(3) A person may, for the purpose of sub-section (1), be detained in a police station or immigration detention area.

363. Section 19(1)(b) and (c) of the *Immigration Act, 2000* (*Act 573*) provides that the High Court may, on an application by the Attorney-General, deprive a person with a right of abode status of that status on the ground that the right was acquired by fraudulent misrepresentation or any other illegal or irregular means; or the holder of the status no longer qualifies under the Act. Section 20(2) of *Act 573* provides that subject to section 19 of that Act, the Director may, during the validity of a permit or visa granted to a person to enter or remain in Ghana, revoke the permit on grounds of fraudulent misrepresentation or concealment or any other illegal practice. He may also revoke the permit if the conditions governing the permit have been breached, or impose new conditions in relation to that permit. In all cases the Director must take reasonable steps to communicate the notice of revocation, and new conditions to the person concerned.

364. Section 28(3) of *Act 573* provides that 'a work permit issued to a person shall specify the employer by whom that person is to be employed and the holder shall not, without the consent in writing of the Committee, engage in any form of paid employment or in any business or professional occupation in Ghana, other than the particular employment, business or professional occupation specified in the work permit'. Thus a breach of a condition specified on a work permit may constitute a ground for revocation of that permit. According to section 20(3) of *Act 573*, where a permit is revoked and notice is given and the holder of that permit is present in Ghana, the holder may not remain in Ghana after will be removed from Ghana in accordance with the provisions of the *Immigration Act*. Following removal the person is prohibited from re-entering Ghana temporarily, or, in the case of a prohibited immigrant, permanently. If the holder of the revoked permit is outside Ghana, the holder is prohibited from re-entering Ghana temporarily, or in the case of a prohibited immigrant, permanently.

365. Sub-sections 4–6 of section 20 of the *Immigration Act* provide that a person who enters or re-enters or remains in Ghana in contravention of an order made under this section, commits an offence and is liable on summary conviction to a fine of not less than fifty penalty units or to a term of imprisonment of no less than three months or more than one year. Where a permit is revoked, the revocation applies to a person whose name is endorsed in the permit, the spouse of the holder of the permit where the spouse was issued a permit in consequence of the issuing of a permit to the other spouse, and any dependant of the holder of the permit who is not a citizen of Ghana. Notification of a revocation order to the holder of the permit constitutes notification to the persons mentioned in the immediately preceding sentence.

366. According to section 34 of the *Immigration Act, 2000 (Act 573)* foreign nationals who:

(1) remain in Ghana for a period exceeding three months must register with the nearest immigration office;
(2) fail to comply with sub-section (1) commit an offence and are liable on summary conviction to a fine not exceeding 250 penalty units, to a term of imprisonment not exceeding twelve months, or to both the fine and the term of imprisonment.

367. Section 35 of the *Immigration Act* makes certain persons liable to deportation. Sub-section (1)(b)(iii) provides that 'a foreign national is liable to deportation if“[he is] found by a Court to be in Ghana without a valid permit, or any of the conditions on which the permit was granted has been broken.”' Where a Court makes such a finding, the Court shall report the finding in writing to the Minister. Under section 36 the Minister may, by executive instrument, order the deportation of a person liable to deportation. The order may be made subject to conditions imposed by the Minister and may include the dependants of the person to be deported if the Minister so directs.

368. The effects of a deportation order are stated in section 37 of the *Immigration Act* as follows:

(1) A person to be deported shall leave Ghana in accordance with the requirements of the deportation order and shall so long as the deportation order is in force remain out of Ghana.
(2) A person who enters Ghana when a deportation order made against that person is in force commits an offence and is liable on summary conviction to a term of imprisonment not exceeding five years and may be deported without a further deportation order being made.
(3) Where a person to be deported is serving a sentence of imprisonment, that person shall, unless the Minister otherwise directs, complete the sentence.

Section 41(1) of *Act 573* provides for the recovery of deportation expenses as follows: 'the Director may apply money or property that belongs to a person to be deported in payment of deportation expenses'.

Part VIII. Access to Self-Employed Activities

Chapter 1. Overview of Applicable Legislation

369. Section 18(1)(c) of *Immigration Act, 2000 (Act 573)* provides that 'a person with indefinite residence status or a person with right of abode status is entitled to work in Ghana as self-employed or as an employee without a work permit'. Thus once a person qualifies for an indefinite residence right or a right of abode status in Ghana, that person no longer needs a work permit to work in Ghana as self-employed person or as an employee.

370. Section 27(3) of *Act 573* provides that the Minister may issue a work permit to a person who is not a prohibited immigrant, a visitor, tourist, transit passenger or student, and who satisfies the Committee that the person who wishes to enter Ghana in order to take up work or employment is qualified to work or undertake employment in the trade, business or calling in respect of which the application is made; the taking up of employment generally benefits Ghana; is a lawfully resident in Ghana; and is qualified to work as an employee or a self-employed person.

371. Enterprises of foreign immigrants are governed by two main investment legislative acts, namely, the *GIPC Act, 2013 (Act 865)* and the *Free Zones Act, 1995 (Act 504). Act 865* provides incentives intended to attract both local and foreign investors. The main targets under *Act 865*, however, are foreign investors. Section 27 of *Act 865* reserves some activities for Ghanaians exclusively (*see* paragraph 40 *supra*). Section 28 of *Act 865* provides foreign capital investment minimum requirements for an enterprise in which foreign participation is permitted (*see* paragraph 41 *supra*). *Immigrant quotas* are based on the paid-up capital of a foreign enterprise under section 35 of *Act 865* (*see* paragraph 42 *supra*). The *Free Zones Act, 1995 (Act 504)* also deals with promoting investment, especially in the manufacturing sector, with the aim of exporting the bulk of the products, and provides several rules for the participation of foreign investors in Free Zones.

372. Section 6 of the *Internal Revenue (Registration of Business) Act, 2005 (Act 684)* provides categories of self-employed persons for the purpose of fixing fees for registration of a business. The Commissioner of Internal Revenue may determine categories of business of self-employed persons and the registration fees payable by those categories. Where there is any doubt as to whether a business falls in one cat egory or the other, this is resolved by the Commissioner. These categories are also relevant for the payment of taxes (*Internal Revenue Act, 2000 (Act 592)*, the *Income Tax (Standard Assessments) Instrument, 1974 (L.I. 974)*, etc.).

373. Section 45 of the *Social Security Act, 1991 (PNDCL 247)* defines a 'self-employed person' as a person who does not have any other employer and works on that person's own account. Section 20(1)(c) of the *Social Security Act, 1991 (PNDCL 247)* provides that that Act applies to all self-employed persons, who opt to join the Scheme. As the Social Security Act does not explicitly exclude foreigners, it appears that it applies to a self-employed foreigner who opts to join the Scheme. Where a member has ceased to be employed, that member may continue to pay the monthly contribution at the rate paid by a self-employed person (section 20(2) of *PNDCL 247*). Section 22(4) of *PNDCL 247* provides that the rate of a contribution to be paid by a self-employed person is 17.5% of any income for the month from the profession, vocation, business or occupation of that person. The *Social Security Act* has been revised by the *Social Security Act, 2009 (Act 766)* which pegs the monthly contributions of self-employed persons at 13.5%. Thus, with effect from 2010, those who opt to join the Scheme as 'Voluntary Contributors' under *Act 766* pay 13.5% rate, while those under PNDCL 247 pay 17.5% rate.

Chapter 2. Conditions for Entitlement to Work in the Country as a Self-Employed Person

374. The main conditions which apply to those who work as self-employed person include capital requirements, processing relevant registration documents, including business or enterprise registration and participation in permissible foreign enterprises. Section 27 of the *GIPC Act, 2013 (Act 865)* excludes certain enterprises from foreign participation and reserves them for Ghanaians exclusively (*see* paragraph 40 *supra*). Section 28 of *Act 865* provides foreign capital investment requirements for enterprises in which foreign participation is permitted (*see* paragraph 41 *supra*). Section 35 of *Act 865* deals with *immigrant quotas* on the basis of paid-up capital of a foreign enterprise (*see* paragraph 42 *supra*).

375. Other conditions that apply when establishing one's own enterprise are found in sections 21(1) and 23 of *Act 865*, which prescribe as a requirement the prior incorporation or registration of such enterprises at the Registrar General's Department in accordance with the *Companies Code, 1963 (Act 179)* or any other laws as are relevant to the establishment of the enterprise. Section 22 of *Act 573* mandates the registration of enterprises in which foreign participation is permitted with the GIPC, after incorporation or registration but before commencement of operations. The Centre shall, within five working days from the date of receipt of the completed registration forms, register the enterprise if it is satisfied that all relevant documents for registration are in order; the minimum foreign equity capital requirement has been complied with; and the fees required for registration have been paid. Registration with the Centre must be renewed every two years.

376. The *Free Zones Act, 1995 (Act 504)*, provides some conditions for those, including foreigners, who want to develop free zones or set up free zone enterprises. Section 8 of *Act 504* prescribes the following qualifications for a person who wishes to develop Free Zones; the person must be a registered body corporate and have acquired the requisite license for such development.

According to section 8 – *Qualification of Free Zone Developers:*

1. No person shall—
   a. develop;
   b. manage; or
   c. develop and manage a free zone unless it is a body corporate registered under the *Companies Code, 1963 (Act 179)* or a partnership registered under the *Incorporated Private Partnership Act, 1962 (Act 152)*.
2. The body corporate or partnership shall be licensed to develop, manage, or develop and manage the free zone under this Act.

377. Section 12 of *Act 504* further outlines the conditions that need to be satisfied in order to establish a free zone enterprise. Several other provisions in *the Free Zones Act, 1995* (Act 504) contain administrative rules and procedures regulating the licensing, sub-contracting by developers and the import and export of products manufactured in free zones. Section 12 of *Act 504* provides that no person shall carry on a trade, business or industry within a free zone unless it is registered under the *Companies Code of 1963* or the *Incorporated Private Partnership Act of 1962* and they are licensed to carry out that trade, business or industry. Such duly registered and licensed companies are referred to as free zone enterprises.

378. Sections 15–17 of *Act 504* deal with the application, the granting and the conditions for licenses to develop a free zone or operate an enterprise in a free zone. An application for a license to develop, manage or establish a free zone enterprise must be in writing; submitted to the Secretariat of the Free Zones Board; specify the zone to be developed or managed or both or the trade, business or industry for which the license is required; and shall be accompanied by any other information required by the Board. The Board responds to the application within twenty-eight working days of receipt. The license may authorize the development, the management or both of a free zone, or the carrying out of a trade, business or industry within the free zone. No license shall be granted to carry out the business of banking, unless the applicant is also registered and licensed under the *Banking Law of 1989*, or the business of insurance, unless the applicant is registered under the *Insurance Law of 1989*. The license is issued under the signature of the Chairman of the Board. The license sets out the conditions regarding employment skills, development, impact on the environment, creation of job opportunities and degree of export orientation as the Board deems appropriate.

379. Under section 18 of *Act 504*, the Free Zones Board may revoke a license where it is satisfied that there has been a breach of a condition attached to it. It must give the licensee at least fourteen working days' notice of its intentions and must consider any representations made to it by the licensee. The Board may, upon request of the licensee and at any time, change the conditions attached to the license. The Board must, pursuant to section 19 of *Act 504*, establish and maintain a register of licenses granted under that Act. For each license, the following information must be recorded: the name of the licensee and the zone to be developed, or managed or both, or the trade, business or industry to which the license relates. The register is kept by the Board and is open for inspection by the public subject to a fee as determined by the Board. According to sections 20 and 21 of *Act 504*, no licensee may transfer a license without the prior approval of the Board. A licensed developer may sub-contract the management, control and promotion of the free zone development in the declared area by applying for a license for any sub-contractor. This license application is accompanied by the executed sub-contract.

380. Sections 21–23 of *Act 504* provide that import and export laws in force in Ghana shall not apply to trade in and out of free zones unless they have been made applicable by that Act or regulations adopted detailing the rules in the Act. The imports of a free zone developer, sub-contractor or enterprises into a free zone or single-factory zone are exempted from direct and indirect taxes and duties. The Minister may by legislative instrument authorize the sales of up to 30% of the annual production of goods and services of a free zone and single-factory zone enterprise to the national customs territory. Sales of goods from free zone enter prises or single-factory zones to the national customs territory are considered as imports and are subject to the rules and regulations relating to imports into the national customs territory. Damaged or rejected goods or samples may be sold by the free zones and single-factory zones to the national customs territory. Such goods are considered as part of 30% of the annual production in the free zones and single-factory zones authorized to be sold to the national customs territory and, as such, are subjected to the applicable duties and taxes. The Minister's legislative instruments provide the penalties for any contravention of the rules.

381. Under section 24 of *Act 504*, the sale of goods and services by a domestic enterprise from the national customs territory to enterprises in the free zone and single-factory zone is classed as exports. A domestic enterprise can benefit from export incentives available to a national exporter and does not need an export license for the sale of goods and services to enterprises in the free zone or single-factory zone. A free zone or single-factory zone enterprise may purchase goods and services sold by a domestic enterprise with local currency obtained through the conversion of foreign currency through the banks or licensed foreign exchange bureaux. An authorized officer of any of the revenue services, a police officer or an officer authorized by the Minister may, in the discharge of their official duties, pursuant to section 25 of *Act 504*, at any time enter and inspect buildings, aircrafts, ships, boats or vehicles in a free zone. While exercising his powers of entry or inspection, he must produce his authorization upon request. Any person who obstructs or attempts to obstruct his entry commits an offence punishable by a maximum of six-month prison sentence or a fine of USD 1,000 or its cedi equivalent, or to both.

Chapter 3. Sanctions Against Illegal Exercise of Self-Employment

382. Section 18 of the *Free Zones Act, 1995 (Act 504)* empowers the Free Zone Board to revoke licences of licensees. The Free Zones Board may revoke a license where it is satisfied that there has been a breach of a condition attached to it. It must give the licensee at least fourteen working days' notice of its intentions and must consider any objections made to it by the licensee. The Board may, upon the request of the licensee and at any time, change the conditions attached to the license. Section 39 of the *Free Zones Act, 1995 (Act 504)* provides sanctions for offences by bodies corporate. The Free Zones Act imputes responsibility for an offence committed by a body corporate to its directors and officers and, when committed by a partnership, to every partner. A person may not be convicted of an offence if it is proven that the act was committed without his personal knowledge or connivance and that he exercised due diligence to prevent the commission of that offence.

383. Section 41(2) of the *Free Zones Act* provides that the Minister may, by legislative instrument, make regulations providing penalties for contravention of the provisions of this Act which may not exceed a twelve-month prison sentence, a fine of 1,000 penalty units or both. The *Free Zone Regulations of 1996* provide for the revocation of a license where the Free Zone Board is satisfied that the licensee has contravened any condition attached to the license. The licensee must be given at least fourteen working days' notice of the Board's intention to revoke the license and the reasons for the revocation. He must have an opportunity to make objections to the Board and have those objections considered by the Board.

384. Regulation 6 of the *GIPC Instrument of 2005* sanctions illegal self-employment. It provides that the Investment Promotion Centre shall cancel an approval that has been obtained on the basis of fraud, intentional or negligent misrepresentation, or where an approval has been assigned without the Investment Promotion Centre's prior written consent. Sanctions may be imposed where an approved enterprise applies a benefit obtained under this instrument for purposes other than those for which the benefit was conferred, or fails, without reasonable documented cause, to submit a report required by this instrument after thirty working days, where written notice of the default has been given, and finally, where an enterprise fails, without reasonable cause, to commence operations within the time stipulated in the approval. As part of these sanctions the Investment Promotion Centre may decide to suspend or cancel the approval, assess taxes or other charges in respect of which benefits have been granted to the enterprise, or recommend the application of sanctions or penalties to the Commissioners of the Customs, Excise and Preventive Service (CEPS) and the Value Added Tax (VAT) for an act or omission which also constitutes an offence under the provisions of their respective governing laws.

385. Sections 40 and 41 of the *GIPC Act, 2013 (Act 865)* provide for offences and penalties. It is an offence for an enterprise to which *Act 865* applies to contravene a provision of that Act. Enterprises must allow an officer or designated agent of the Centre to enter its premises to perform the monitoring functions of the Cen tre. Any enterprise that refuses to admit such an officer or agent commits an offence punishable by a fine of not less than 500 penalty units and not more than 1,000 penalty units. In the case of a continuing offence, an additional fine of not less than twenty-five penalty units and not more than fifty penalty units for each day that the offence continues can be imposed on the perpetrator.

Chapter 4. Legal Remedies and Procedural Safeguards

386. Regulation 14(2) of the *Free Zone Regulations, 1996 (L.I. 1618)* provides that a licensee must be given at least fourteen working days' notice of the Free Zone Board's intention to revoke his license and the reasons for the revocation. He must have an opportunity to make objections to the Board and have those objections considered by the Board.

387. Section 18(3) of the *Free Zone Act, 1995 (Act 504)* provides that in revoking a licence, the Free Zone Board must give no less than fourteen working days' notice of its intentions to the licensee and must consider the objections made to it by the licensee. Again, section 39 of the *Free Zones Act, 1995 (Act 504)* in providing sanctions for offences by bodies corporate, indicates that a person may not be convicted of an offence under sub-section (1) if it is proven that the act constituting the offence was committed by another person and without the personal knowledge or connivance of, and that due diligence was exercised by, that person to prevent the commission of the offence having regard to the circumstances.

388. As noted earlier, Articles 23 and 33 of the *1992 Constitution* provide detailed remedies and procedures for the enforcement of human rights and the revision of administrative decisions. Immigration officials and persons or authority vested with discretionary power when exercising these powers must be fair and candid, and in no way act arbitrary, capricious or biased either by resentment, prejudice or personal dislike, but in accordance with the due process of law and published regulations (Article 296). For example, Article 23 of the *1992 Constitution* of Ghana provides that 'administrative bodies and administrative officials shall act fairly and reasonably and comply with the requirements imposed on them by law, and persons aggrieved by the exercise of such acts and decisions shall have the right to seek redress before a court or other tribunal'.

389. All persons therefore have a right to appeal against any decision affecting their right to work in Ghana, as provided for by sections 46 and 47 of the *Immigration Act, 2000 (Act 573)*. According to section 46 of *Act 573* which deals with the submission of petitions, a person, other than a prohibited immigrant, aggrieved by a refusal to grant or renew a permit, the revocation of a permit or a repatriation ordered made by an immigration officer, may submit a petition to the Minister within seven days of the action and the Minister must, subject to sub-section (3), take the appropriate action. Sub-section (3) provides that the Minister, in determining a petition under sub-section (1), is assisted by a committee comprising of a representative of the Attorney-General not below the rank of a Senior State Attorney, who acts as the chairman of the committee; a representative of the Minister for Foreign Affairs not below the rank of a Director; and one other person appointed by the Minister who is not an officer or employee of the Immigration Service.

390. Section 47 of *Act 573* makes it clear that a petition to the Minister under section 46 of that Act does not stay the action which has been petitioned against. However, the *Immigration Regulations* provide the conditions under which a per son may be permitted to stay in Ghana pending the hearing of a petition made by that person. Section 51 of *Act 573* vests the Minister with 'Residual Powers' where the Minister may revoke or waive a visa, a permit, an entry condition and any other requirements if required by the national interest, compassionate circumstances or any other reasonable ground.

391. Section 18(1)(c) of *Immigration Act, 2000 (Act 573*) provides that 'a person with indefinite residence status or a person with right of abode status is entitled to work in Ghana as self-employed or as an employee without a work permit'. However, under section 15(3) of *Act 573*, 'where a person is granted an indefinite residence status and that person is absent from Ghana for more than twelve consecutive months, the indefinite resident status is automatically lost'. Thus, a person who has automatically lost his indefinite residence status will automatically lose all the rights that go with that status, including the entitlement to work in Ghana as self-employed person or as an employee without a work permit. All these notwithstanding, a person who loses an indefinite residence status under Section 15(3) of *Act 573* may apply to the Director for reinstatement, but the application shall be treated as a new application subject to the conditions determined by the Director under section 15(4) of *Act 573*.

392. Section 34(1) of the *Human Trafficking Act, 2005 (Act 694)* provides that, notwithstanding the provisions in section 21 of the *Immigration Act, 2000 (Act 573*) (on the removal of an illegal immigrant), a trafficked person who is in Ghana unlawfully may remain in Ghana throughout the period of a legal investigation and the prosecution of a trafficker and that the Human Trafficking Management Board makes the arrangements for the repatriation of the trafficked person upon completion of the legal proceedings against the trafficker. Under section 3 of the *Refugees Law, 1992 (PNDCL 305D*), a refugee may be detained or expelled for reasons of national security or public order, unless expulsion is to a country where the refugee has reason to fear persecution.

393. Section 19 of *Act 573* entitled 'High Court may revoke the right of abode status' provides in sub-section (1) that the High Court may, on an application by the Attorney-General, deprive a person with a right of abode status of that status on the ground that (a) the activities of that person are inimical to the security of the State or prejudicial to public order, public health, morality or public interest; (b) the right was acquired by fraudulent misrepresentation or any other illegal or irregular means; or (c) the holder of the status no longer qualifies under the Act. Thus when the Director of Immigration seeks to revoke the permit of a person on grounds of fraudulent misrepresentation, concealment, or any other illegal practice, or because the conditions governing the permit have been broken, or merely wants to impose new conditions in relation to that permit, he has to follow the procedure set out in section 19(1) of *Act 573,* by making an application to the High Court. Moreover, the Director has to take reasonable steps to communicate the notice of revocation or the new conditions to the person concerned.

394. The revocation notice is usually as set out in *Form K* of the *Immigration Regulations, 2001 (L.I. 1691)*. Such notification is required under section 19(3) of that act. Under section 19(5) it also serves as the notification to the persons whose names are endorsed in the permit, the spouse of the holder of that permit where the spouse was issued the permit as a consequence of the issuing of the permit to the other spouse, and any dependants of the holder of that permit who are not citizens of Ghana.

395. Several other procedural safeguards are applicable in such matters. Under Ghana's *1992 Constitution*, a petitioner has a right to be represented by a lawyer of his choice. Moreover, although a petition to the Minister under Article 46 of the *1992 Constitution* does not stay the action which has been petitioned against, the petitioner may be permitted to stay in Ghana pending the hearing of the petition made by him (Article 47 of the *1992 Constitution*). All these procedural rules and the right to petition the Minister under Article 46 *1992 Constitution* provide very good procedural safeguards to foreigners.

Selected Bibliography

Addison, E.K.Y. 'The Macroeconomic Impact of Remittances'. In *At Home in the World? International Migration and Development in Contemporary Ghana and West Africa*, edited by T. Manuh. Accra: Sub-Saharan Publishers, 2005.

Addo, N.O. 'Foreign African Workers in Ghana'. *International Labor Review* 109 (1974):47–68.

Adebusoye, Makinwa Paulina. 'Geographic Labour Mobility in Sub-saharan Africa'. IDRC Working Papers on Globalization, Growth and Poverty. Ottawa: Int'l Development Research Centre, 2006.

Adepoju, A. 'Fostering Free Movement of Persons in West Africa: Achievements, Constraints, and Prospects for Intraregional Migration'. *International Migration* 40, no. 2 (2002):3.

Adepoju, A. 'International Migration in Africa, South of the Sahara'. In *International Migration Today*, edited by Reginald Appleyard. Vol. I, Trends and Prospects Paris: UNESCO, 1988.

Adepoju, A. 'Migration in sub-Saharan Africa'. Curr. Afri. Issues, 37, (2008).

Adepoju, A. 'Patterns of Migration in West Africa'. In *At Home in the World: Contemporary Migration from Ghana and West Africa,* edited by T. Manuh. Accra: Sub-Saharan Publishers, 2005.

Adepoju, A. *International Migration Within, to and from Africa in a Globalised World.* Accra: Sub-Saharan Publishers, 2010.

Adjei, Elizabeth. 'From Origin to Destination: Policy Perspective on Female Migration: Ghana case study'. Presented at the UN Symposium on International Migration and Development. Turin, 2006, African Centre for Human Development, *The Little Ghanaian Slaves Cry for Help: A Report on Child Trafficking in Ghana*. Accra: Print Solutions Ltd, 2002.

Agarwal, Seema et al. *Bearing the Weight: The Kayayoo – Ghana's working Girl Child.* Legon: Centre for Social Policies Studies, 1997.

Ammassari, Savina. 'From Nation-Building to Entrepreneurship: The Impact of élite Return Migrants in Côte d'Ivoire and Ghana', Paper presented at the International Workshop on Migration and Poverty in West Africa(Sussex, 2003).

Anarfi J.K & S.O. Kwankye with Ofosu-Mensah Ababio and Richmond Tiemoko. 'Migration from and to Ghana: A Background Paper'. DRC Working Paper C-4 (2003).

Selected Bibliography

Anarfi, J.K, K. Awusabo-Asare & Nsowah-Nuamah. 'Push and Pull factors of International Migration'. Country Report: Ghana. Eurosat Working Papers 2000/E (10). European Commission, Statistical office of the European Communities (2000).

Anarfi, J.K. 'Historical Overview of Migration Within the ECOWAS Sub-region'. Ch.19 in *Migration Research Study in Ghana*. (Volume 1. *Internal Migration*; Volume 2- *International Migration*. Twum-Baah, K.A., J.S. Nabila & A.F. Aryee, eds., Accra1995), Project undertaken by Ghana Statistical Service (GHA/88/PO4) with Social Sector Policy Unit, MFEP (GHA/88/PO3.).

Anarfi, John et al. 'Migration from and to Ghana: A Background Paper'. Migration DRC Working Paper: No.C4. Sussex: Development Research Centre on Migration, Development Research Centre on Migration, Globalization, and PovertyUK: University of Sussex,2003, www.sussex.ac.uk/migration/.

Apt, Nana Araba et al. *Listening to Girls on the Street Tell Their Own Story: What will Help Them Most?* Legon: Center for Social Policies Studies, 1997.

Asiedu, A. 'Some Benefits of Migrants' Return Visits to Ghana. Paper presented at international workshop on migration and poverty in West Africa(University of Sussex, Brighton, UK2003).

Awumbila M., T. Manu et al. *Migration and Mobility in Ghana: Trends, Issues, and Emerging Research Gaps* Accra: Woeli Publishing Services, 2011.

Awumbila, M. 'The Gendered Face of Poverty: Female Porters and Adaptive Responses to poverty in Urban Ghana'. In *The Changing face of Poverty in Ghana*, edited by K. Awusabo-Asare. et al. Trondheim: Department of Geography and Resource Development. NTNU, 2005.

Awumbila M., T. Manu, et al. Migration: Ghana Country Paper. Accra: University of Ghana Centre for Migration Studies, 2008

Benneh, E.Y. 'The International Legal Regime and Migration Policies of Ghana, the ECOWAS Sub-Region and Recipient Countries'. In *At Home in the World? International Migration and Development in Contemporary Ghana & West Africa,* edited by T. Manuh. Accra: Sub-Saharan Publishers, 2005.

Berry, S. 'Social Institutions and Access to Resources'. *Africa* 59.11989: 41–55.

Berry, S. *No condition is Permanent*, Madison: University of Wisconsin Press, 1993.

Black, R, R. King & R. Tiemoko. 'Migration, Return and Small Enterprise Development in Ghana: A Route Out of Poverty?' Migration DRC Working Paper: No. 9. (Sussex: Development Research Centre on Migration, Globalization, and Poverty2003). www.sussex.ac.uk/migration/.

Black, Richard et al. 'Migration, Return and Small Enterprise Development in Ghana: ARoute Out of Poverty?', Migration DRC Working Paper: No. 9. (Sussex: Development Research Centre on Migration, Globalization, and Poverty 2003a). www.sussex.ac.uk/migration/.

Black, Richard. 'Migration and Pro-poor Policy in Africa', Migration DRC Working Paper: No. C6. (Sussex: Development Research Centre on Migration, Globalization, and Poverty2004). www.sussex.ac.uk/migration/.

Boyd, M. 'Family and Personal Networks in International Migration – Recent Developments and New Agendas'. *International Migration Review*, 23 no. 3 (1989): 638–670.

Bump, M. *Ghana: Searching for Opportunities at Home and Abroad.* Washington DC: Migration Information Source, 2006. www.migrationinformation.org.

Caldwell, J.C. *African Rural-Urban Migration: The Movement to Ghana's Towns.* Canberra: Australian National University Press, 1969.

Carrington, W.J. & E. Detragiache. 'How Extensive is the Brain Drain?'. *Finance and Development* 36, no. 2 (1999):46–49.

Castles, S. 'The Factors that Make and Unmake Migration Policies'. *International Migration Review* 38, no. 3 (2004): 852–884.

Cholewinski, R., R. Perruchoud& E. Macdonald. *International Migration Law—Developing Paradigms and Key Challenges.* Cambridge: Cambridge University Press, 2007.

Clark, G. *Onions Are My Husband: Survival and Accumulation in a West African Urban Market.* Chicago: University of Chicago Press, 1994.

Codjoe, S.N.A. 'Migrant Versus Indigenous Farmers: An Analysis of Factors Affecting Land Use in the Transitional Agro-Ecological Zone of Ghana, 1984-2000'. *Danish Journal of Geography*106, no. 1 (2006): 103–113.

Coombe, R. & P. Stoller. 'X Marks the Spot: The Ambiguities of African Trading in the Commerce of Black Public Sphere'. *Public Culture* 15 (1994): 249–274.

Devyver, A. 'In Search of Greener Pastures: A Study of Strategies used in West African Migration to Western Europe'. Unpublished thesis submitted to the University of Ghana(Legon2005).

Diko J. & A.G. Tipple. 1992. *Migrants Build at Home: Long Distance Housing Development by Ghanaians in London. Cities* 9, no. 1. Elsevier,1992,288–294.

Docquier, F. & A. Marfouk. 'Measuring the International Mobility of Skilled Workers (1990-2000)', Policy Research Working Paper Series: No. WPS3381(DC: World Bank2004).

Eades, J.S. *Migrants, Workers and the Social Order.* London and NY: Tavistock Pub, 1987.

Eades, J.S. *Strangers and Traders: Yoruba Migrants, Markets and the State in Northern Ghana.* Edinburgh: University of Edinburg Press for the International African Institute, 1993.

EU Ghana Migration Profile. Accra: European Commission Delegation, 2006.

European Union, *The Cotonou Agreement.* europa.eu, 2006.

Findley, S.E. 'Migration and Family Interactions in Africa'. In Family, Population and Development in Africa, edited by Adepoju. London/New Jersey: Zed, 1997.

Garcés-Mascarenas, Blanca. *Research on Trafficking and Forced Labour among West African Migrants in the Netherlands.* Amsterdam: Institute for Migration and Ethnic Studies, 2005.

Ghana Immigration Service (2006). (in Manuh, T. *Ghana Migration Profile.* Ghana: A Study for the Ministry of Foreign Affairs, 2006.)

Ghana Immigration Service (2008). Migration to and from Ghana (Compilation from 2000 to 2008 (in Quartey, Peter. Migration in Ghana: A Country Profile. A Report Prepared for and published by the International Organization for Migration) (Geneva: Switzerland, 2009)

Ghana Immigration Service (2009). (Annual Report for 2008: Analysis of Immigration Data) (Compiled by GIS Management Information System/Statistical Unit, Ghana, 19/02/2009)

Selected Bibliography

Ghana Statistical Service. 'Migration Research Study in Ghana'. In *Internal Migration in Ghana*, edited by K. Twum-Baah, J.S. Nabila& A. F. Aryee. Vol. 1,Accra: Ghana Statistical Service, 1995.

Ghana Statistical Service. *2000 Population and Housing Census Report- Summary Report of Final Results, Accra,* 2002.

Ghana Statistical Service. *2000 Population Data Analysis Report,* Vol.1 Policy implications of Population Trends, 2005.

Ghana Statistical Service. *Ghana Living Standards Survey (Round 5) Report*, 2005/6, 1999.

Ghana Statistical Service. *Ghana Living Standards Survey (Round 5) Report*, 2005/2006, 2008.

Ghana Statistical Service. *Population Census Report*, Accra: Ghana Statistical Service, 1960.

Ghana Statistical Service. *Population Census Report*, Accra: Ghana Statistical Service 1970.

Ghana Statistical Service. *Population Census Report*, Accra: Ghana Statistical Service 1984.

Goodwin-Gill. *The Refugee in International Law*,UK: Clarendon Press, 1985, 69–100.

Hart, K. 'Migration and Tribal Identity among the Frafra of Ghana'. *Journal of Asian and African Studies,* 6 (1971): 21–36.

Hart, K., 'Rural-Urban Migration in West Africa' In *Migrants, Workers and the Social Order,* edited by J.S. Eades. London and New York: Tavistock Publications, 1987.

Hasim, Iman M. 'Children's Independent Migration from Northeastern to Central Ghana', Migration DRC Research Report(Sussex: Development Research Centre on Migration, Globalization and Poverty 2005b). www.sussex.ac.uk/migration/.

Hasim, Iman M. 'Exploring the Linkages Between Children's Independent Migration and Education: Evidence from Ghana', Migration DRC Working Paper: No.12. (Sussex: Development Research Center on Migration, Globalization and Poverty 2005a). www.sussex.ac.uk/migration/.

Higazi, Adam. 'Ghana Country Study', Paper published as a Part of the Report on Informal Remittance Systems in Africa, Caribbean and Pacific(Oxford University: ESRC Centre on Migration Policy and Society (COMPAS)2005).

Hill, P. *The Migrant Cocoa Farmers of Southern Ghana: A Study in Rural Capitalism.* Cambridge: Cambridge University Press, 1970,

Indexmundi. 'Ghana, Net Migration Rate'. Indexmundi,2003, www.indexmundi.com.

International Labour Organization. *Combating Trafficking in Children for Labour Exploitation in West and Central Africa: Synthesis Report*. Geneva: International Labour Organization. 2001.

International Organization for Migration. *Projects in Ghana.* IOM,2006,www.iom.int.

Killick, T. 'Labour, A General Survey'. In *A Study of Contemporary Ghana, The Economy of Ghana*, edited by Walter Birmingham, I. Neustadt & E.N. Omaboe. Vol. I. London: Allen and Unwin, 1966.

Konadu-Agyemang, Kwadwo. 'Travel Patterns and Coping Strategies of Ghanaian Immigrants in Toronto'. *Ghana Studies* 2 (1999):13–34.

Kwankye, S.O., J.K. Anarfi, C.A. Tagoe & A. Castaldo. 'Independent North-South Child Migration in Ghana: The Decision-Making Process, Working Paper T-29, Development Research Centre on Migration, Globalisation and Poverty(University of Sussex, UK 2008).

Litchfield, Julie et al. 'Migration and Poverty Reduction: Evidence from the Ghana Living Standards Survey'. Migration DRC Working Paper: No.10. Sussex: Development Research Centre on Migration, Globalization and Poverty. Working Paper No. 10, 2003. www.sussex.ac.uk/migration/.

Lucas, R.E.B. & O. Stark. 'Motivations to Remit: Evidence from Bostwana'. *Journal of Political Economy* 93 (1985):901–18.

Manuh, T. & R. Asante.'Reaping the Gains of Ghanaians Overseas: An Evaluation of the Home Coming Summit of 2001'. In *At Home in the World? International Migration and Development in Contemporary Ghana and West Africa*, edited by T. Manuh. Accra: Sub-Saharan Publishers, 2005.

Manuh, T. 'Diaspora, Unities and Market Place: Tracing Changes in Ghanaian Fashion'. *Journal of African Studies* 16, no. 1 (1998):13–19.

Manuh, T. 'Ghanaian Migrants in Toronto Canada: Care of Kin and Gender Relations'. *Research Review*, Institute of African Studies, University of Ghana, New Series, Vol. 17, No. 2, 2001.

Manuh, T. 'Migration from Africa: Challenges, Opportunities and Policy Responses'. Keynote address at Expert Meeting on International Migration and National Development. The Netherlands, 2006.

Manuh, T. *An 11th Region of Ghana? Ghanaians Abroad*. GAAS: Inaugural Lecture, 2006.

Manuh, T. *Ghana Migration Profile*. Ghana: A Study for the Ministry of Foreign Affairs, 2006.

Manuh, T., R. Asante & J. Djangmah. 'The Brain Drain in the Higher Education Sector in Ghana'. In *At Home in the World? International Migration and Development in Contemporary Ghana and West Africa,* edited by T. Manuh. Accra: Sub-Saharan Publishers, 2005.

Manuh, Takyiwaa. 'International Migration and Development in Ghana'. In *International Migration and Academic Freedom Notes from Colloquium Participants*: 1-2, edited by Global Colloquium of University Presidents. New York: Colombia University in the City of New York, 2005.

Manuh, Takyiwaa. 'Introduction: Contemporary Ghanaian Migrations'. *Ghana Studies* 2 (1999):5–11.

Manuh, Takyiwaa. 'This Place is Not Ghana': Gender and Rights Discourse among Ghanaian Men and Women in Toronto'. *Ghana Studies* 2 (1999a):77–95.

Massey, D., J. Arango, G. Hugo, A. Kouaouci, A. Pellegrino & J. Taylor. 'Theories of International Migration: A Review & Appraisal'. *Population & Development Review* 19, no. 3 (1993):431–466.

Mazzucato, V., B. van den Boom & N.N. Nsowah-Nuamah. 'Origin and Destination of Remittances in Ghana'. In *At Home in the World? International Migration and Development in Contemporary Ghana and West Africa*, edited by T. Manuh. Accra: Sub-Saharan Publishers, 2005.

Selected Bibliography

Mazzucato, Valentina. 'Global Migration Perspectives. Ghanaian Migrants' Double Engagement: A Transnational View of Development and Integration Policies', GCIM Working Papers: No. 48. Geneva: Global Commission on International Migration, 2005, www.gcim.org.

Miescher, Stephan F. et al. 'Been-to Visions: Transnational Linkages among a Ghanaian Dispersed Community in the Twentieth Century'. *Ghana Studies* 2 (1999):57–76.

Ministry of Foreign Affairs and Cooperation of the Kingdom of Morocco. Euro-African Ministerial Conference on Migration and Development. Rabat, 10–11 July, 2006. www.iri.edu.ar/publicaciones_iri/anuario/CD%20Anuario%202006/Africa/Rabat1.pdf.

Mohammed, Janet Adama. *Report on Baseline Study on Human Trafficking and Forced Labour in Northern Ghana.* Accra: International Labour Organization, 2005.

Morgenthau, R.S. 'Strangers, Nationals and Multinationals in Contemporary Africa'. In *Strangers in African Societies,* edited by William Shack & Elliott Skinner. Berkeley, Los Angeles: University of California Press, 1979, 105–122.

Nabila, J.S. 'Rural Migration and Its Implications for Rural Development in Ghana'. In *Rural Development in Ghana*, edited by C.K. Brown. Accra: Ghana Universities Press, 1986,75–89.

Nabila, J.S. *Urbanisation in Ghana, Population Impact Project, Department of Geography and Resource Development.* Legon: University of Ghana, 1988.

Nyonator, F. & D. Dovlo. 'The Health of the Nation and the Brain Drain in the Health Sector'. In *At Home in the World? International Migration and Development in Contemporary Ghana and West Africa*, edited by T. Manuh. Accra: Sub-Saharan Publishers, 2005.

Oguaa, Emelia & et al. *Study on Children in Fishing in Yeji Fishing Communities.* Accra: Ghana NGO Coalition on the Rights of the Child, 2005.

Olofson, H. 'Yawon Dandi: A Hausa Category of Migration'. *Africa.* 46, no.1 (1976): 66–79.

Owusu, G. & J. Agyei. *Changes in Land Access, Rights and Livelihoods in Peri-Urban Ghana: The Case of Accra, Kumasi and Tamale Metropolis.* Study Conducted as Part of Land Tenure Policy and Reform Project by ISSER, University of Ghana, 2008.

Owusu-Ankomah, Papa. 'Emigration from Ghana: A motor or Brake for Development?', Paper presented at 39th Session of the Commission on Population and Development. (NY: UN www.un.org, 2006).

Peil, M. 'Ghanaians Abroad'. *African Affairs* 94, no. 376 (1995):345–67.

Quartey, P. 'Migration and Development: Challenges and Opportunities for Sending Countries. Ghana Country Case Study', A Report Prepared for the German Marshal Fund of the USA. (Washington: July 22–262006).

Quartey, Peter. Migration in Ghana: A Country Profile. A Report Prepared for and published by the International Organization for Migration) (Geneva: Switzerland, 2009)

Quartey, Peter. 'Shared Growth in Ghana: Do Migrant Remittances Have a Role?', CORNELL/ISSER/World Bank International Conference on Shared Growth in Africa. Accra, July 21–22, 2005. http://www.isser.org/86%20Quartey.pdf.

Quartey, Peter. 'The Impact of Migrant Remittances on Household Welfare in Ghana'. Final Report Submitted the African Economic Research Consortium. (Nairobi 2006a). http://www.csae.ox.ac.uk/conferences/2006-EOIRPI/papers/csae/Quartey.pdf.

Republic of Ghana Children's Act, 1998 (Act 560) Accra: Government Printer.

Republic of Ghana Citizenship Act, 2000, (Act 591) Accra: Government Printer.

Republic of Ghana Concessions Act, 1939 (Cap 136) [enacted as Concessions Ordinance, 1939(19)] Accra: Government Printer.

Republic of Ghana *Constitution of Ghana, 1992* Accra: Government Printer.

Republic of Ghana Criminal Offences Act, 1960 (Act 29) [originally enacted as Criminal Code] Accra: Government Printer.

Republic of Ghana Diamonds Act, 1972 (N.R.C.D. 32) Accra: Government Printer.

Republic of Ghana Free Zone (Amendment) Act, 2002 (Act 618) Accra: Gov't Printer.

Republic of Ghana *Free Zones Act, 1995 (Act 504)* Accra: Government Printer.

Republic of Ghana *Ghana Investment Promotion Act, 2013 (Act 865)* Accra.

Republic of Ghana *Identity Cards Decree, 1972 (N.R.C.D. 129)* Accra: Gov't Printer.

Republic of Ghana *Identity Cards Regulations, 1972 (L.I. 794)* Accra: Gov't Printer.

Republic of Ghana *Immigration Regulations, 2001 (L.I. 1691)* Accra: Gov't Printer.

Republic of Ghana *Immigration Service Law, 1989 (PNDC Law 226)* Accra.

Republic of Ghana Immigration Service Regulations, 1997 (L.I. 1636) Accra.

Republic of Ghana Internal Revenue Act, 2000 (Act 592) Accra: Government Printer.

Republic of Ghana Labour Act, 2000 (651) Accra: Government Printer.

Republic of Ghana Small Scale Gold Mining Act, 1989 (PNDCL 218) Accra.

Republic of Ghana *Social Security Regulations, 1973 (L.I. 818)* Accra: Gov't Printer.

Republic of Ghana. *Human Trafficking Act* (Act 694) Accra: Gov't Printer, 2005.

Republic of Ghana. *Immigration Act, 2000* (Act 573) Accra: Government Printer, 2000.

Republic of Ghana. *Refugee Law, 1992* (PNDCL 305D) Accra: Gov't Printer, 1992.

Riisøen, Kari Hauge et al. *Travel to Uncertainty: A Study of Child Relocation in Burkina Faso, Ghana and Mali*. Oslo: Allkopi AS, 2004.

Rimmer, D. *Staying Poor: Ghana's Political Economy 1950-1990.* Oxford: Pergamon, 1993.

Sabates-Wheeler, Rachel & et al. 'Tackling Poverty-Migration Linkages: Evidence from Ghana and Egypt', Migration DRC Working Paper: No.14. Sussex: Development Research Center on Migration, Globalization and Poverty2005. www.sussex.ac.uk/migration/.

Schildkrout, E. 'Ethnicity, Joking and Kinship among Urban Immigrants in Ghana'. In *Migration and Ethnicity,* edited by Betty du Toit and Helen Safa. The Hague: Mouton, 1975.

Schildkrout, E. *People of the Zongo: The Transformation of Ethnic Identities in Ghana.* Cambridge, New York: Cambridge University Press, 1978.

Secretariat of the African, Caribbean and Pacific Group of States (ACP). *Migration and mobility of ACP nationals within Europe.* Paris: CG/F, 2004.

SEND. One nation, One people, One destiny? The Ghanaian Diaspora's Contribution to National Development using Diverse Channels. An action research study of resource mobilization by Ghanaians in the Diaspora to three regions in Ghana. Unpublished report prepared as part of the 'Hello Africa: Shifting Power, Tackling Poverty by connecting Africa and the African Diaspora'. Funded by Comic Relief, the UK. Accra, 2004. (May) (www.afford-uk.org/documents).

Shack, W. & E. Skinner (eds.). *Strangers in African Societies*. Berkeley, Los Angeles: University of California Press, 1979.

Shack, W. 'Open Systems and Closed Boundaries: Stranger-Host Relations in Independent Africa'. In *Strangers in African Societies*, edited by W. Shack & E. Skinner. Berkeley, Los Angeles: University of California Press, 1979,37–50.

Sudarkassa, N. 'From Strangers to Alien: The Socio-political History of the Nigerian Yoruba in Ghana, 1900-1970'. In *Strangers in African Societies,* edited by W. Shack & E. Skinner. Berkeley, Los Angeles: University of California Press, 1979.

Sudarkassa, N. 'The Economic Status of the Yoruba in Ghana Between 1900-1970'. *Nigerian Journal of Social Studies.* 17 (1975): 91–125.

Takyi, B.K. 'The African Diaspora: A Socio-Demographic Portrait of the Ghanaian Migrant Community in the USA'. *Ghana Studies* 2 (1999):35–56.

Tete, S. 'Narratives of Hope? Displacement Narratives of Liberian Refugee Women and Children in The Gomoa-Budumburam Refugee camp in Ghana. Unpublished Master's Thesis, Trondheim University, NTNU, 2005.

Twum-Baah, K.et al., *Migration Research Study in Ghana*, Accra: Ghana Statistical Service, 1995, 1.

Twum-Baah, K. 'Volume and Characteristics of International Ghanaian Migration' In *At Home in the World? International Migration and Development in Contemporary Ghana and West Africa*, edited by T. Manuh. Accra: Sub-Saharan Pub, 2005.

UNHCR. *Ghana*.2006b, www.unhcr.org.

UNHCR. *Ghana*.2006c, www.unhcr.org.

UNHCR. *Global Report–Ghana.* New York: UNDP, 2008,249–253.

UNHCR. *Liberia Operations*.2006a, www.unhcr.org.

USCR. US Committee for Refugees. *World Refugee Survey 2006*.2005,www.refugees.org.

USOMCT. Trafficking in Persons Report, Ghana: USOMCT, 2006, www.state.gov.

Van Hear, N. *New Diaspora: The Mass Exodus Dispersal and Regrouping of Migrant Communities.* London: UCL Press, 1998.

Vujicic M, P. Zurn, K. Diallo& M. Dal Poz. *The Role of Wages in Slowing the Migration of Health Care Professionals from Developing Countries. Department of Health Services Provision*, Geneva: World Health Organisation, 2004.

Williams, V. *Regional Cooperation and the Benefits of Migration for Development in Southern Africa.* In *How Migration Can Benefit Development,* edited by K. Tamas & J. Palme. Stockholm: Institute for Futures Research, 2006.

Zachariah, K.C. &J. Conde. *Migration in West Africa: Demographic Aspects.* Oxford: Oxford University Press for the World Bank, 1981.

Zlotnik, Hanik. *Migrants' Rights, Forced Migration and Migration Policy in Africa*,2003, available in pumprinceton.edu/pumconference/papers/6-zlotnik.pdf.

Index

The numbers here refer to paragraph numbers.

Index

Index

Made in the USA
Monee, IL
18 October 2026

66041393R10103